Games
As Learning Tools
A GUIDE FOR EFFECTIVE USE

Dorothy D. Sullivan
University of Maryland

Beth Davey
University of Maryland

Dolores P. Dickerson
Howard University

Instructo/McGraw-Hill
Paoli, Pennsylvania 19301

Editorial Direction: Roberta Richards
Editorial Assistant: Marcia Tosh
Art Director/Cover Design: Gilbert Lieberman
Designer/Illustrator: M. Jane Smyth
Typographer: Mary Casatelli

Copyright © 1978 by Instructo/McGraw-Hill, Inc. All rights reserved. Printed in the United States of America. No part of this publication may be reproduced, stored in a retrieval system, or transmitted, in any form or by any means, electronic, mechanical, photocopying, recording, or otherwise, without the prior written permission of the publisher. For information regarding permission write Instructo/McGraw-Hill, Inc.

10   9   8   7   6   5   4

Library of Congress Cataloging in Publication Data
Sullivan, Dorothy D
   Games as learning tools.

   Bibliography: p.
   Includes index.
    1. Educational games. I. Davey, Beth, joint author.
II. Dickerson, Dolores P., joint author. III. Title.
LB1029.G3S94   371.3   77-12424
ISBN 0-07-082059-7

Table of Contents

Chapter 1: Games as Learning Activities   1
What kinds of games can you use for learning activities? 2
How do games help students learn? 5
Which type of learning games will work in my classroom? 12

Chapter 2: Getting Started with Games   13
*How can I help parents understand that games can be worthwhile
in the learning process?* 13
*How do I get students to understand that skills and concept development
are essential aspects of learning games?* 15
When should I use learning games in my classroom? 16
How do I introduce games to the students? 21
How do students play learning games independently? 21
What special guidelines would help me with teacher-directed games? 22
How shall I organize the learning games for classroom use? 22
Should students select their games to play? 27
Are there any special tips for organizing games for learning activities? 29

Chapter 3: Using Games Diagnostically   31
Why use games for diagnosis? 32
How can games be used diagnostically? 33
*What special considerations should you keep in mind when
using games diagnostically?* 35

Chapter 4: Designing and Making Games   41
Where do I start? 41
Where do I start in developing learning games? 43
Are there basic guidelines I should follow in designing games? 47
How can I construct games so that they will last? 52
How can commercial games be adapted to learning games? 54
Where can I get help for making games? 55
Have workshops proved helpful for constructing games? 56

Chapter 5: Formats/Directions/and Basic Game Guidelines   59
How to use this chapter 60
Passive Game Formats 61
Active Game Formats 90
Which games should I use? 94

Chapter 6: Game Ideas   95
How to use this chapter 96
Vocabulary 98
Concepts and Facts 109
Word Analysis 120
Graphic-Symbolic 132

Chapter 7: Other Sources For Game Ideas   143
Game Index 150
Subject Index 153

FOREWORD

This book grows from our commitment to the concept that classroom learning should and can be a positive experience for kids. Using games in the classroom is one approach that we feel has proved successful in this respect.

The ideas presented here for designing games and implementing their use have come from many sources. Ideas first came from our work with children in the University of Maryland Reading Clinic. As our work with games was refined in terms of appropriateness and effective ways of working with them, statewide workshops for teachers of all grade levels were held. In turn, ideas were shared with us by workshop participants. Therefore the material presented comes from the reality of classroom and clinic usage. The ideas are workable, ready for adaptation to your classroom situation, and endorsed by teachers, parents, and most importantly — students.

This book is dedicated to the many people who felt the need for it and encouraged its development, sharing with us the belief that learning can be fun.

D.D.S.
B.D.
D.P.D.

Chapter 1

Games As Learning Activities

What kinds of games can be used for effective learning? How do games help students learn?

Learning can be both stimulating and pleasurable. As teachers seek new ways to facilitate the learning process there is growing interest in how games can help students learn. In recent years publishers have increased the variety of learning games for all grade levels and subject areas. Teachers' use of games, however, has usually been sporadic with minimum emphasis on them other than having them available for students. These games might have been used steadily for several months after their arrival in the classroom, but after their novelty has worn off they often remain unused on a shelf gathering dust, with parts missing. The use of educational games too frequently is relegated to rainy days along with rummy, checkers, and dominoes. With the arrival of teacher aides in the classrooms some games have been put to greater use. In the meanwhile, teachers of remedial programs in reading and math have been using learning games successfully as planned instrucional activities to help disabled learners acquire basic skills and concepts. It is now recognized that teachers might also achieve similar results with students by utilizing games as regular classroom activities. We believe that consistent and regular use of games in the classroom can make a difference in student learning and attitude.

It is the purpose of this book, therefore, to put you into the learning-games business, so-to-speak, to guide you in developing your own games, and in the use of both commercial and teacher-made games as viable learning experiences for students. This chapter describes the rationale for using learning games. Chapter 2 shows you how to get started using games as learning activities, how to organize classroom learning activities to include games, and ways to adapt games to age, maturity, interests, and skills development of students. Chapter 3 presents ideas for using games diagnostically. Chapter 4 provides

Games As Learning Tools

guidelines and procedures for designing your own games and adapting commercial games for skills reinforcement. It also discusses ways that teachers and schools have found the necessary help to make games. Chapter 5 describes in detail basic game formats in terms of directions for play and guidelines that have been found helpful in using the respective types of games for learning activities. Chapter 6 presents specific ideas that can be adapted for development of basic content skills in different subject areas and at various instructional levels. Chapter 7 provides an annotated bibliography of other sources of games ideas.

What kinds of games can you use for learning activities?

All games that are used in learning activities have a common characteristic. Learning games have been defined as activities in which players use a body of knowledge or set of skills as resources in their competition with other players (DeVries and Edwards, 1973, p.308).

There are a number of so-called educational games on the market described in games and activities books that are not learning games by our definition, involving competition. They might more appropriately be labeled as learning activities, both independent and teacher directed. This misconception of learning games is evident from proposed 'game' ideas teachers have considered making in games-construction workshops. They have taken their cues from learning activities that they have seen labeled as games. In games for learning **chance** plays a dominant role in the competition of winning (or losing). Players are not eliminated because of "not knowing" as in the old spelling bees. The major focus on games for learning is its provision for maximum peer learning as participants interact in the game situation. Although competition is a necessary component of games, it is utilized within a positive framework through its stimulating effects and opportunities for cooperative effort in the fun of playing. Learning games provide practice and reinforcement as well as — opportunities for content and skills application in fun settings.

Games for learning may be labeled as passive, simulation, or active. A learning game calls for the player to perform some content or skill task when it is his or her turn. The ability to perform an educational task is involved in each player's progress.

Games As Learning Activities

Passive Games

Passive games include bingo, concentration, dominoes, checkers, card and board games. An example of a card game to reinforce phonics would be one that uses sets of picture or picture-word cards focusing on initial consonant or consonant blend sounds, medial, long or short vowels, or final consonants. These phonics card sets would then be played as *Go Fish* or *Rummy*. A teacher-made board game with an Indi-500 race track would have task cards calling for players to utilize a variety of skill reinforcement tasks. The game could call for locating words in a newspaper story that are examples of different word attack skills:

- a word with a prefix meaning "not"
- a VC-CV word
- a word with a past tense ending
- a word with a plural possessive
- a word with a prefix and a suffix
- a three-syllable word

The same game board might also be used to reinforce key vocabulary words from a social studies unit. Students draw from a vocabulary deck when it is their turn. If a student can define the word he or she draws correctly, that player then moves the number of spaces on the board that he or she has thrown on the die.

Games As Learning Tools

Simulation Games

Simulation games are considered an extension of passive games and are usually based on principles and content of some "external reality," such as social and political dilemmas. Carefully planned simulations involve participants in real-life problem-solving situations and frequently include role playing experiences. They have been used

successfully with students at **all** grade levels with many content areas. Comprehension of content concepts and acquisition of functional learning skills are major goals developed through simulation games. However, because of the unique characteristics and complexities of process-oriented simulation games, they will not be included in this book.

Active Games

Active games are those games that are most often thought of as being physical education-type games and include relays, circle games, and tag games with such physically oriented tasks as running, tossing or throwing, catching, skipping, or jumping. A subject-area concept or skill is practiced in the course of participating in the active game situation.

Games As Learning Activities

Such games have particular appeal to elementary grade students. For younger students there can be a circle game called *Rainbow* (see page 135) while *What Is-It-Relay;* (see page 138) is geared for older students. Both of these games which focus on vocabulary demonstrate how various age groups can use active games for learning academically oriented skills.

How do games help students learn?

Students need many "experiences" with the content and skills introduced in the school curriculum. They need many exposures to a word before it is recognizied instantly and consistently to become a part of their sight vocabulary. Students need practice in applying word attack, vocabulary, or other skills to new and meaningful situations before they achieve independent mastery of these skills. Learning games can provide the needed repetition for skill mastery without the negative effect of drill-type activities (Wilson, 1972, p. 206). Games enable students to obtain the necessary reinforcement and skill application experiences in a setting that is highly motivating and pleasurable. The effectiveness of games for learning is based on basic principles of learning as well as child growth and development.

Games Help: By Their Use of High Interest and Motivation of Students

Games enable students to obtain the necessary reinforcement and skill application experiences in a setting that is highly motivating and pleasurable. Almost all students like to play games. When physical activity is included in the game structure, the interest seems to be heightened. The research of Dickerson (1975) supports the positive effect of passive and active games on developing sight vocabulary among young children. Furthermore many teachers we have worked with in games-construction workshops report similar interest and enthusiasm from their students. With games, reinforcement activities can be structured to be fun-oriented rather than drill-oriented to move students to independent mastery of skills. When placed in positively-oriented game situations, the student's own high interest and motivation work toward the acquistion of knowledge and skills. This effect makes for a more satisfying teaching-learning experience.

Games As Learning Tools

Games Help: By Their Use of Feedback and Reinforcement of Student Performance

Games are particularly unique in providing feedback and reinforcement, an essential in learning activities. A typical game task might require the player to:

- give another word that rhymes with the word the teacher pronounces
- identify the prefix or suffix in a word drawn from the card pile
- match two cards according to the objects pictured on them
- identify a statement card as fact or opinion
- identify two words on a card as antonyms or synonyms

In order that the player move or take a turn as leader, the student must be able to perform a specific skill task. Rules of the game might include getting the help of a teammate to complete the task. The student either moves ahead or waits until it is his or her next turn to proceed. The player, therefore, has immediate feedback as to the correctness of the response. Such knowledge of results is considered a strong and important factor in learning (Bilodeau and Bilodeau, 1961, pp. 243-270). Immediate feedback is particularly effective when it is provided as soon as responses are made (Dolinsky, 1966, p. 13). Since games serve as reinforcement activities for skills previously introduced and with which the student has some degree of success, it is found that most players can provide appropriate responses for the game tasks.

Several aspects of reinforcement are operating in the games approach to learning. The positive nature of the learning activity serves as a reinforcement in itself. It also becomes important to complete the skill task successfully. In active games an additional motor involvement provides a correspondingly greater number of responses associated with and conditioned to learning stimuli. And finally, the positive orientation of game activities provides more generalized reinforcers to the responses of the player (Sullivan and Humphrey, 1973, p. 81).

Games As Learning Activities

Games Help: By Their Use of the Social Setting to Enhance Learning

Another definition of learning games cites their pleasurable social setting as a factor facilitating their effectiveness as a learning medium (Humphrey and Sullivan, 1970, p. 11). While learning is an individual matter, it can take place effectively in a social setting in which the group can serve as a stimulus to the individual, and individuals within a group can learn from each other. Furthermore, when watching students participating in learning games we observe that each student not only makes a response when it is his or her turn, but he or she also keeps track of the accuracy of the other players' responses. The use of game rules that give students opportunities to seek help utilizes the same principle as does the use of a buddy system in playing games or working on learning centers.

Games Help: By Individualizing Learning Activities

From questions teachers ask it appears that many envision total classes participating in learning games — particularly active games. There needs to be a better understanding of the role of games in providing for student learning experiences within the classroom. True, some learning games provide the entire class with additional experiences which relate to curriculum content or skills. In fact, such games should be considered highly desirable **if** they can be fun for and meaningful to all the students in that group. An example of this use of a learning game would be a relay race matching social studies vocabulary words with their definitions. A second example would be a tag game with prefix and suffix matching. By their very nature many passive games limit the number of players. The major exception to this is the bingo-type game. Unfortunately, some teachers believe that such games must involve the whole class, and must be teacher-directed. As a result they overwork the bingo-type game, and, indeed, they use this type of game exclusively for learning comprehension and reinforcement. Some teachers have learned to increase the number of participants in board games using football, soccer, or hockey as their theme. They have four or five students representing each team instead of a single-player or 'buddy' team. Determination of a correct response is a team decision. This type of team participation is useful with weaker students as they learn during the team process of determining a correct response. Team play usually requires some type of supervision.

Games As Learning Tools

However, most learning games lend themselves to independent learning situations. You may elect to have students use learning games independently as you are working with a group. You might also set aside specific periods of time during a week when all students are involved in playing learning games. You are then able to observe and have individual conferences with the students about the skills they are working on or the games they are playing. In each of these situations you may make a selection of the skills to be worked on by your students based upon your diagnosis of the skill strengths and needs. If you are striving to have students involved in decisions regarding their own learning, their self-evaluation may direct their choices as to content and skills to be reinforced in the games they select to play. Such choice-making implies that you have a variety of games that are suitable for, or can be adapted to, the content or skill in which your students need practice. With such a collection of games, students and skills can be matched. Individual student needs can be better met.

Just as individual strengths and needs vary for different students, so does the amount of repetition required for independent skill mastery by individual students. A **collection** of games can be utilized most effectively to provide sufficient variety of learning activities to hold student interest when developing or reinforcing concepts or skills. Individual interests should also be considered as you build a collection of games. Games reflecting the sports, hobbies, or other special interests of the students you are working with indicate your awareness of them as 'persons' as well as students. Also, students have a range of preference as to types of games they play. With a variety of games students can then select the type of game they enjoy playing.

Your awareness of the unique needs and capacities of your students will enable you to select and develop types of games that are particularly suited to your students' maturity, interests, and curriculum needs. A learning disability group may need a simple, highly-structured one-action relay game (see page 104). A total class of high achievers might be capable of handling complicated tasks in a more physically varied and involved relay race. You may need to balance strong and weaker students on relay teams or board games teams to provide for individual differences. Card games can be made simple or complex by the rules and tasks set up for the same sets of cards. Students functioning at different reading levels can play a game together effectively by having each student use his or her own individual set of word cards, or

Games As Learning Activities

Language Experience Approach story, basal reader, or library book during the game. So, if a student draws a task card telling the player to find a word that has the same beginning sound as in **boy** the student turns to his or her own reading material to locate such a word. Being able to so individualize learning games enables you to implement an instructional program using each student's strengths and needs.

Games Help: By Their Use of Student Self-Direction Through Self-Evaluation

Other recent classroom innovations, such as learning centers and contracting, are structured to encourage students to become independent and self-directed learners (Waynant and Wilson, 1974, pp. 1-4; Wilson and Gambrell, 1975, pp. 3-5; Waynant, 1977, p. 4). One aspect of choice-making involves the decision of students to use a learning game for concept or skills reinforcement. Classroom games also call for students to take an active part in making choices related to the games they play, to evaluate their own performance, and to make decisions as to further learning activities.

Initially, you will be selecting the content or skill to be practiced in the games chosen by the students. There may be times when you will need to adjust student choice of game because several students request to use the same game during the same period. Or, a particular game may require a kind of supervision that you may not be able to arrange at that time.

While there will be times when you group students to play a particular game that focuses on a specific content or skill, at other times you will find that the use of learning games in the classroom involves the development of a **variety** of active and passive-type games appropriate to the maturity of your students and to their curriculum. Concentration, checkers, dominoes, card, board, and bingo games adapted to content

Games As Learning Tools

and skills reinforcement activities should be available to students for their selection. There is, therefore, not just one game to reinforce one specific skill, but several. Furthermore, most games can be used to reinforce several skills. A collection of games provides a broader spectrum of learning experiences for students. Another form of choice-making involves choosing partners or agreeing to play a game together.

After students have finished playing their games you should spend a few moments with them getting their reactions to the game. You will be drawing from them such suggestions as:

"I need to look at the words more carefully."

"It took too long to play. Maybe we should use two dice so we can move farther each turn, or work in teams."

"I don't like going back so much. Couldn't we make new chance cards? We could make them so you got extra turns or moved ahead more often, not always losing turns and going back."

These are meaningful problem-solving situations for students which encourage them to take responsibility for constructive learning experiences.

Self-evaluation procedures are also built into the use of learning games. Games, to be learning activities, must incorporate procedures whereby students are fully aware of the specific content or skills they are working on in the game they are playing. Games lend themselves naturally to specific, behaviorally-stated educational objectives. The following are samples of skill-oriented game tasks:

Game Task	Skill Objective
When I hold up a word card, the first person on each relay team is to run to the board. This person writes another word that rhymes with that word. A point is scored for the first team to write a correct rhyming word.	Rhyming and initial consonant substitution
Two cards with pictures of words that begin with the same consonant blends make a pair. They may be pictures of the same or different words.	Recognition of initial consonant blends

Games As Learning Activities

After playing a game it is a simple matter for you to discuss with the students how easily they were able to handle the specific content or skill tasks used. Students should be encouraged to assess their degree of mastery and whether or not they feel they need additional practice. Students appear more willing to evaluate their performance realistically when the prospect of additional learning activities are interesting and pleasurable and games rather than tedious paper and pencil activities. Student decision-making as to their own learning becomes a reality while students also become more content-and-skill oriented in the process.

Which type of learning games will work in my classroom?

You will need to pick and choose.

Each type of learning game has its own particular contribution to make to the curriculum. You will find the active game (a circle, stunt or tag game) is particularly useful in working with the physically-oriented primary grade children. You will learn, too, that a relay race or a tossing or pitching game may also serve as a welcome change-of-pace activity for intermediate-grade students. Active games need not always be relegated to the playground or multi-purpose room. They can be played in self-contained classrooms or within open-space class areas. At the University of Maryland Reading Clinic such active games have been used effectively in open-space areas where many groups are working. Teachers of regular open-space school situations have reported similar success.

The various formats of passive games easily lend themselves to the classroom setting, from card games and dominoes for primary grades to bingo, concentration, and checkers in the intermediate and middle grades and secondary levels. Board games can reflect the full spectrum of maturity, interests, and curriculum content of K-12 students. As you become more comfortable with offering learning games as part of the regular classroom activities you will broaden the variety of games you offer students. You will learn what, and how many games can be played independently with how many students while you are carrying on a teacher-directed small group activity. You will find you can supervise an active game with one group of students while the remaining students are working independently. Your use of games as learning activities can be as varied as the use of learning centers and contracts; they lend themselves equally well to the unique needs of each group or individual.

Games As Learning Tools

Selected Bibliography

Bilodeau, Edward A. and Ina Bilodeau. "Motor Skill Learning," Annual Review of Psychology. Palo Alto: California, 1961, pp. 243-70.

Davey, Beth. "Cognitive Styles and Reading Achievement," Journal of Reading, Vol. 20, No. 2 (Nov.) 1976, pp.113-120.

DeVries, D.L. and K.J. Edwards. "Learning Games and Student Teams: Their Effect on Classroom Process," American Education Research Journal, X, 1973, pp. 307-18.

Dickerson, Dolores. "A Comparison of the Use of the Active Games Learning Medium with Passive Games and Traditional Activities as a Means of Reinforcing Recognition of Selected Sight Vocabulary Words with Mid-Year First Grade Children with Limited Sight Vocabulary." Unpublished doctoral dissertation, University of Maryland, 1975.

Dolinsky, Richard. Human Learning. Dubuque, Iowa: Wm. C. Brown Co., 1966.

Gambrell, Linda and Robert M. Wilson. Focusing on the Strengths of Children. Belmont, California: Fearon Publishers, 1973.

Humphrey, James H. and Dorothy D. Sullivan. Teaching Slow Learners Through Active Games. Springfield, Illinois: Charles C Thomas, 1970.

Sullivan, Dorothy D. and James H. Humphrey. Teaching Reading Through Motor Learning. Springfield, Illinois: Charles C Thomas, 1973.

Waynant, Louise and Robert M. Wilson. Learning Centers . . . A Guide for Effective Use. Paoli, Pennsylvania: The Instructo Corporation, 1974.

Waynant, Louise. Learning Centers II . . .Practical Ideas for You. Paoli, Pennsylvania: Instructo/McGraw-Hill, 1977.

Wilson, Robert M. Diagnostic and Remedial Reading for Classroom and Clinic, 2nd edition. Columbus: Charles E. Merrill, 1972.

Chapter 2

Getting Started With Games

How do you enlist support of games for learning? How do you organize effective classroom use of learning games?

First of all, when using games as learning activities in the classroom it is essential that both parents and students understand that this is *another* and *valid* approach to learning. You should plan to inform parents as to the skills and concept development orientation of the games approach to learning. This type of information will help gain parent confidence and support while you use these activities.

How can I help parents understand that games can be worthwhile in the learning process?

You may want to use a portion of your meeting with parents at the beginning of the school year to demonstrate some games and other activities such as learning centers and contracts that you plan to use for skills and concept development. This might be done as a part of the initial school sponsored parent and teacher meeting of the year. You might have a collection of various types of games, centers, and contracts on display for parents to examine and ask questions about. You need to explain what skills will be reinforced with these activities. You can show parents the value of these activities as effective alternatives to traditional drill and practice-type activities in skills and concept development. At this time you might also solicit volunteer help from parents for constructing games and other teacher-designed materials for the classroom as well as for working directly with students. It has been found that some parent volunteers are more comfortable preparing instructional materials than in working directly with students and welcome opportunities to contribute time to the schools in a non-instructional capacity.

Games As Learning Tools

Another way to inform parents of the use of learning games might be done by sending a letter to parents at the beginning of the school year. Some teachers have described in such letters the several types of learning activities they plan to use during the year. They also invite parents to visit the classroom to familiarize themselves with these alternative approaches to learning. Other teachers (throughout the year) have sent letters home with game ideas for reinforcing certain skills in order that parents might also help students with their learning.

In the University of Maryland Reading Clinic the role of games as learning activities is always explained during the orientation session to parents at the beginning of each clinic. Parents are also invited to help make the games that will be used in the clinic. A daily workshop has evolved from their enthusiasm in helping to construct games. Each game that is completed in the workshop is demonstrated by the clinician so that the parents will see how the game is used for skills reinforcement. They are also invited to watch students use the game. Some parents invited other parents to the game workshop with the intent of setting up similar workshops in their schools in order to help teachers to get games into regular classrooms. Such enthusiasm obviously came from the value these parents placed on games as effective learning activities for their own children.

Getting Started With Games

Such awareness on the part of parents as to the value of games is essential, particularly with the increasing emphasis on teaching "the basics." Unfortunately teaching the basics is being construed as moving the desks back into rows and taking pleasure out of the learning process by returning the students to traditionally dull drill-type activities. The recognition that learning activities such as games, contracts, and centers can provide necessary drill for skill reinforcement and concept development is essential if parents and educators alike are going to accept these activities as valid contributions to the curriculum. Needless to say, after giving games a fair trial, some of the less enthusiastic teachers in games workshops have joined the ranks of the most enthusiastic supporters of games as learning activities. The enthusiastic response of their students to this approach to skills practice convinced them of the value of games as learning activities.

How do I get students to understand that skills and concept development are essential aspects of learning games?

Students, as well as parents, need to be aware of the skills being reinforced in the games they are playing. They need to recognize that games offer opportunities for mastering skills or developing concepts as well as providing change-of-pace fun activities. This can be achieved in two ways: when the game is initially introduced, the skill that will be worked on can be discussed; and secondly, during the self-evaluation session following the playing of the game, the skill can be considered. After playing games, students are encouraged to assess whether they need further practice with the specific skills being reinforced or the concepts being developed through the games. In this way students come to appreciate how games make learning pleasurable. This understanding is particularly important if a time comes when you feel that students are forgetting to play games without disrupting other groups with their noise, are getting careless in handling the games, or are simply fooling around while playing. Whenever there is a breakdown in good games management, and such problems do occur occasionally, a talk with students about preferring games as fun-oriented learning activities in place of more traditional drill-type assignments usually gets matters straightened out. It is not a hard decision for them to make. Moreover, teachers report that few problems arise in using games; that students seem to appreciate their efforts to provide stimulating and interesting learning activities. They also report that students show definite interest

Games As Learning Tools

in developing new rules and designing new games for skill reinforcement themselves.

When should I use learning games in my classroom?

Learning games may be used as an integral part of the curriculum. Games can be used to provide students with practice in skills you have previously introduced. You may utilize learning games as you would learning centers, workbooks, or dittoed assignments for skills reinforcement through practice and application. Great variation is possible in organizing learning activities using games.

Learning games may serve as independent activities while you carry out small group instruction. Also, you may lead a game with a small group or with the total class to assess how well students are handling particular skills. You may have an aide supervise skill reinforcement through learning games. Peer tutoring can also be used in this way. You may schedule periods during which students are using centers or games while you confer with them individually about their activities and the skills involved. Such use of games as learning activities may take place in self-contained or open-space classrooms, with team teaching or departmentalized situations. Several examples show how the curriculum can be organized to include games as an integral part of learning activities.

In Examples 1a and 1b game activities are worked into independent activities similar to the way centers and the more traditional reinforcement activities are utilized.

Examples 1a

GROUP	9:30 - 10:00	10:00 - 10:30	10:30 - 11:00	11:00 - 11:30	11:30 - 12:00
A	Teacher-Directed Activity	games	non-centers*	centers	total class
B	centers	Teacher-Directed Activity	games	non-centers*	Teacher-Directed Activity
C	non-centers*	centers	Teacher-Directed Activity	games	Activity

(Conferences — 11:30 - 12:00)

*assignments in workbooks, dittoed pages, chalkboard activities

In Example 1a, as an elementary grade teacher within a given period of time you may work with small groups while other students work at center and non-center activities and/or learning games to practice skills

Getting Started With Games

and concepts that you have previously introduced. Centers and games may be assigned or be student-selected, depending upon the degree of self-evaluation and self-direction achieved by the students. You may also devote some time to evaluation by holding conferences with students as to their independent activities for the purpose of planning further learning activities.

Example 1b typifies a four-week unit in a content area. During the first week the teacher's objectives are to assess the information and skill background that students possess. The purposes for the unit are established. The teacher discusses the types of activities available. Three independent research project groups based on student interest are formed by the teacher. In the succeeding weeks each group carries out research preparing their culminating reports.

Example 1b:

Four-Week Unit in a Content Area

50 minute period:
- 5 min. — organize classroom
- 40 min. — class activities
- 5 min. — reorganize classroom

FIRST WEEK ON UNIT

GROUP	Monday	Tuesday	Wednesday	Thursday	Friday
A	Teacher-	Teacher-	unit	Teacher-	library research
B	Directed	Directed	film	Directed	*
C	Activity	Activity		Activity	Teacher-Directed Activity

*learning games/centers reinforcing unit concepts and skills

SECOND WEEK ON UNIT

GROUP	Monday	Tuesday	Wednesday	Thursday	Friday
A	library research	organize report	organize report	GROUP A presents report to class	*
B	Teacher-Directed Activity	library research	TDA follow up assign.		*
C	TDA follow-up assignment	TDA assignment check	*		Conference on Report

(T. Conferences; Teacher-Directed Activity)

*learning games/centers reinforcing unit concepts and skills

Games As Learning Tools

THIRD WEEK ON UNIT

GROUP	Monday	Tuesday	Wednesday	Thursday	Friday
A	Teacher-Directed Activity	TDA follow-up assignment	* ⋮	Group B presents	*
B	organize report	library research	organize report ⋮ Conferences	project report	Teacher-Directed Activity ⋮ *
C	*	library research	organize report ⋮	to class.	Conference on report

*learning games/centers reinforcing unit concepts and skills

FOURTH WEEK ON UNIT

GROUP	Monday	Tuesday	Wednesday	Thursday	Friday
A	* ⋮ T. Conferences	GROUP C presents report to class	Unit Summation Review	Unit Test	Go over test. Discuss research projects
B	* ⋮				
C	organize report ⋮				

*learning games/centers reinforcing unit concepts and skills

In Example 1b, as a content-area teacher, you are using learning games and centers for independent practice on unit concepts and skills. These games and centers can have several dimensions of application of the skills and concepts as well. A learning game and center can be used to reinforce the same key concept or skill. Learning games and centers can foster the application of a key concept or skill in different ways. For example, a key concept or skill might be applied in different contextual situations through a number of learning games and centers. Students can work as individuals and/or as buddies on these learning games and centers. You may utilize a record-keeping system whereby you will be able to be sure that students played the games and completed assigned centers for concept and skill reinforcement.

Throughout this unit, you will work closely with the students on an individual and group basis to monitor progress. The students will be encouraged to evaluate and react to their work on unit skills practiced with the games and centers. In addition to self-evaluation, the students will be encouraged to evaluate and react to the information and presentation of each group. The unit test, another evaluation procedure, would include information presented to the class by teacher and students as well as the concepts and skills developed by the unit games and centers.

Getting Started With Games

Example 2:

GROUP	9:30 - 10:00	10:00 - 10:30	10:30 - 11:00	11:00 - 11:30	11:30 - 12:00
A	Teacher-Directed Activity	centers	non-centers*	Teacher-Directed Activity	Games. T. Conferences Aide supervises game for slower learners.
B	Aide-Directed Game	Teacher-Directed Activity	centers/ non-centers*		
C	peer tutoring centers/ non-centers*	Aide-Directed Game	Teacher-Directed Activity		

*assignments in workbooks, dittoed pages, chalkboard activities

In Example 2 a specified period is utilized for games as learning activities, again with the teacher holding conferences with individual students. Here you are utilizing an aide's services with supervision of learning games. In all these examples there might be a combination of assigned and self-selected skill focus.

Example 3 shows how you may use games with a small group or total class for specific skills application. This offers an alternative way other than tests for assessing how students are handling specific skills.

Example 3:

GROUP	9:30 - 10:00	10:00 - 10:30	10:30 - 11:00	11:00 - 11:30	11:30 - 12:00
A	Teacher-Directed Activity	centers/games	non-centers*	Teacher-Directed Activity	Teacher-Directed Game
B	centers/games	non-centers*	Teacher-Directed Activity		
C	non-centers*	Teacher-Directed Activity	centers/games		

*assignments in workbooks, dittoed pages, chalkboard activities

Here you are having an entire class or one group practice a skill that the students are working on. This might be an active-game relay focusing on such skills as vocabulary development with synonyms and antonyms, dictionary skills, or multiplication facts.

Games As Learning Tools

Learning games may also supplement the curriculum by having them available in the classroom for students to play when their assignments are completed. These learning games are also skill and concept-development oriented. Example 4 shows how games can be utilized as students complete assigned work and contracts.

Example 4:

	Monday	Tuesday	Wednesday	Thursday	Friday
50 Minute Period	Teacher-Directed Activity .... assigned work *	Teacher-Directed Activity .... assigned work *	Teacher works with those students needing extra help **	Teacher-Directed Activity .... assigned work *	Teacher-Directed Activity .... assigned work *

*Learning centers and games may be utilized when students complete assignments.

Example 4 specifically shows how content-area teachers may also utilize learning games as a supplement to the curriculum. Some content-area teachers utilize learning games and centers in these ways.

Learning games and centers are developed for concept and skill reinforcement for each content-area unit. As unit concepts and skills are introduced, you present related games and centers to the students. Introduce the games to the total group and have several students play the game so they can teach other students later. Such supplementary material provides a few students with additional guidance for concept or skill understanding while the rest of the group receives independent meaningful practice and application of the same skills in interesting and highly motivating settings. You are not designating specific games or centers for the students to use in this situation. Rather, students select learning activities for practice and application of concepts and skills based on their own self-evaluation of their strengths and needs.

Getting Started With Games

How do I introduce games to the students?

1. One game should be taught at a time. You will need to work closely with the first players, teaching them the rules. Actually, you should play the game through with them, several times, if necessary. The skills used in the game should be highlighted.
2. It is advisable to begin with able learners. Then, as they become experienced, they pair off with other students. In this way the entire group who will be using the game becomes familiar with the game.
3. A buddy or team of students may function as one player in a game. A less able student may consult with a buddy or team member for help concerning a game task. This may slow down the play but it enables the less able student to remain in the game — and learn in the process.

How do students play learning games independently?

1. Once all students know a number of games, several students may be permitted to sign up to play a game during specified independent work periods. You may assign specific games for certain students to play. Or, students may select a game; you determine the skill to be worked on. At a later time students can be encouraged to identify skill areas they feel they need to work on in learning games.
2. You may limit the number of game groups playing during any given period of time. A game Sign-Up Chart for specific time periods might be useful. As you start using games for learning activities you will be able to determine the most effective arrangements for your group.
3. You may want to have an aide, an able reader, or an older pupil as tutor to help less able students to play a learning game. Arrangements can be made for this at specific time periods.
4. An answer key may be made for some games so that students can check their responses to the game tasks. One student might serve as record keeper for checking answers and keeping score.
5. You may want one student taking responsibility for checking in all games at the end of each period in which they are used. The student should check that the game task cards as well as all game parts are returned in good condition. Each game parts box might have a list on the inside cover of what the game parts include and how many there should be of each. This helps to assure that learning games will be ready for use when needed.

Games As Learning Tools

6. To pace games you may need to adjust the play so that the length of time to complete a game maintains student interest. This may mean using a pair of dice or a spinner with numbers 6-12 to speed up a game, or one die or a spinner with numbers 1-6 to slow down a game.
7. Each day students have used learning games you should spend time conferring with them as to their reactions to the games, problems they may have had playing the game, and ways to improve such situations, and how well they handled the skills or concepts practiced in the game. Gradually you may encourage them to determine if they need further work with the skills or concepts.

What special guidelines would help me with teacher-directed games?

1. Be sure the skill you plan to reinforce is one that each student in the group can handle.
2. When selecting a game, consider the abilities of the students to handle the directions. Game procedures must not be too complex.
3. In relay-type games the groups should be balanced by placing more capable with less able ones. This balance should also be considered when different physical skills are used in active games. Such arranging need not be obvious and does help to provide a satisfying experience for all the students with a more even competition. For example, a leader holds a ball a few seconds longer before tossing it in the air where certain less able students are to respond to a game task such as words being called out that have an initial consonant blend corresponding to the ones they are assigned.
4. Stop playing while interest is high.

How shall I organize the learning games for classroom use?

Organizing games to facilitate their use in the classroom may be done in a number of ways. In starting a collection of games to be used as learning activities you need to identify and list specific skills that can be reinforced through practice. In the elementary grades this would be done in each subject area. You might then use a dual system of coding with colors designating subject areas and a numbering system to identify skill areas. Or, as a content-area teacher, you might use colors to designate skill areas and a numbering system to identify units. The coding system you develop should then be used to label the learning

Getting Started With Games

games and to identify games in a master file. Each game you have developed, either by yourself or a commercial one that you have adapted, should be described briefly on a file card with the code notation of the skill areas reinforced by the game. A master file is kept of the games in order to help you select appropriate learning activities for the students. Some teachers have developed a cross file by skill areas since many games are adapted not only to several skill areas within one subject area, but also to skills in different content areas.

A type of coding system might include the following designations:

Subject Area — Color

Reading-L.A.	yellow
Science	blue
Social Studies	green
Math	red
Business	orange

Content-Area Units — Arabic (science)

Matter	1
Energy	2
Etc.	3

Specific Skill Areas Within Subject (example - reading)

I Phonics
    a - consonants
    b - consonant blends
    c - consonant digraphs
    d - vowels

II Word Attack
    a - vowel letter patterns
    b - syllabication
    c - structural analysis

III Vocabulary
IV Comprehension
V Study Skills

Games As Learning Tools

A master card file entry might look like this:

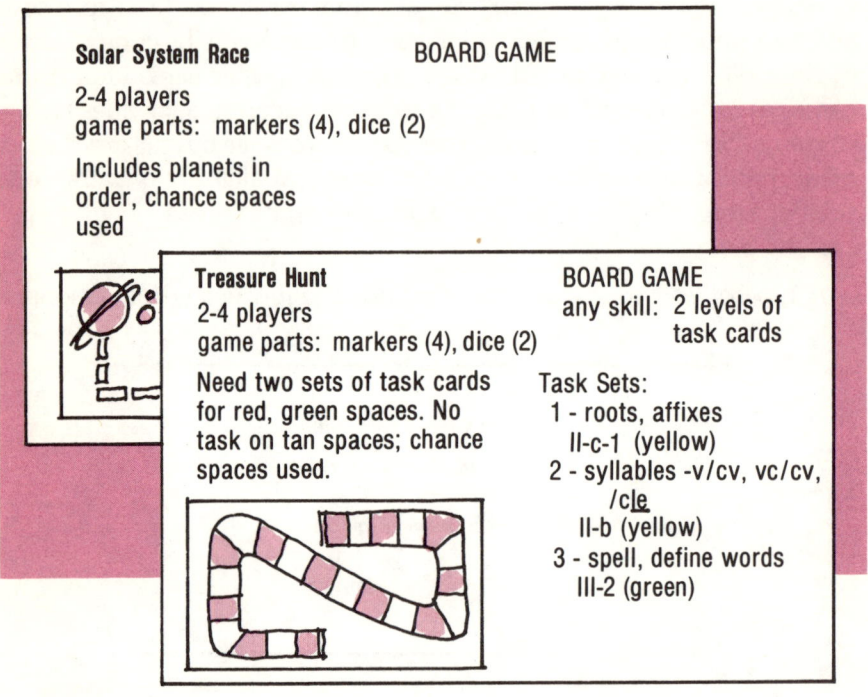

```
Solar System Race            BOARD GAME
2-4 players
game parts: markers (4), dice (2)

Includes planets in
order, chance spaces
used
```

```
Treasure Hunt                BOARD GAME
2-4 players                  any skill: 2 levels of
game parts: markers (4), dice (2)   task cards

Need two sets of task cards  Task Sets:
for red, green spaces. No     1 - roots, affixes
task on tan spaces; chance      II-c-1 (yellow)
spaces used.                  2 - syllables -v/cv, vc/cv,
                                /cle
                                II-b (yellow)
                              3 - spell, define words
                                III-2 (green)
```

The cross-reference card would include:

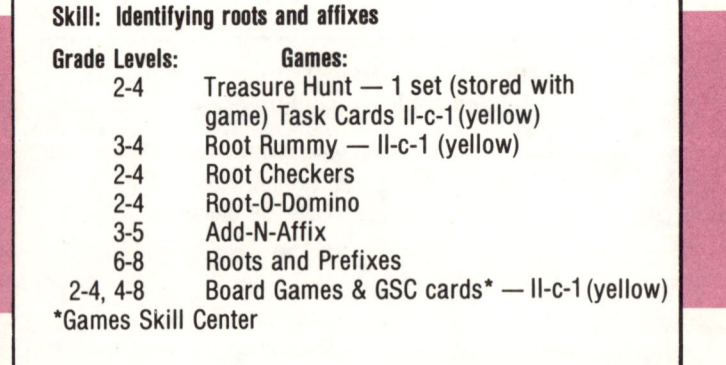

```
Skill: Identifying roots and affixes

Grade Levels:          Games:
    2-4         Treasure Hunt — 1 set (stored with
                game) Task Cards II-c-1 (yellow)
    3-4         Root Rummy — II-c-1 (yellow)
    2-4         Root Checkers
    2-4         Root-O-Domino
    3-5         Add-N-Affix
    6-8         Roots and Prefixes
  2-4, 4-8      Board Games & GSC cards* — II-c-1 (yellow)
*Games Skill Center
```

Additional strategies for differentiating games using file cards are described in Chapter 2, pages 25-27.

Getting Started With Games

In this case you know you have several games specifically designed to focus on identifying roots and affixes. The grade level of words included in the games range from second through eighth grade. Since you designed the games, you also know that you have included words from the students' basal readers, math texts, and social studies and science units. There are sets of task cards in the Games Skills Center area labeled II-c-I (yellow) that students can use in any of the adaptable board games you have in the classroom according to their level of reading achievement.

Games and game parts are labeled according to the coding system you devise. For example, two games, *Checker Blends* (see page 121) and *Blend Search* (see page 122), are limited to a specific skill area. According to our coding system yellow labels, for reading-language arts, are marked I-b, the Roman numeral I to designate the skill area of phonics and -b to indicate that they focus on consonant blends. These labels are put on the game parts boxes for *Checker Blend* and *Blend Search*.

However, games that may be adapted to a number of skills by different sets of task cards are not labeled. Rather, the code labels are attached to the appropriate box or brown envelope used to store each set of task cards and kept in one central storage location. In this way, the skill-oriented task card sets are easily available for use with many games by being kept in a Games Skill Center (GSC). An example of a multi-skill game would be a *Lou Sleuth — Ace Detective* (see page 46) board game that you could design to appeal to middle school students. The game is then played with whatever task cards you select to use, depending on the skill or concept to be practiced. The science and social studies teachers might have made up several sets of unit vocabulary

Games As Learning Tools

words. As the reading-language arts teacher, you asked these teachers to put together these sets; it is your intention to help students increase their vocabulary by reinforcing words they are learning in the various content areas. You have also developed numerous sets of task cards focusing on antonyms, synonyms, prefixes, suffixes, and many others.

These sets are labeled according to the system you have developed:

Task Card Sets	Labels		Skills Orientation
	Color	Number	
science vocabulary	blue	III-1	blue = science III = vocabulary -1 = Unit 1 - Matter
social studies vocabulary	green	III-3	green = social studies III = vocabulary 3 = Unit 3 - Federalists
antonyms and synonyms	yellow	III-(2-4)	yellow = reading-language arts III = vocabulary (2-4) = 2nd to 4th grade level
prefixes and suffixes	yellow	II-c-1(2-3)	yellow = reading-language arts II = word attack c = structural analysis -1 = roots, affixes (2-3) = 2nd -3rd grade level

It is simply a matter then of the students selecting the games they wish to play and your deciding what skills they need to work with. You are able to match individuals and appropriate skills reinforcement activities for them. Likewise, students themselves can come to decisions as to skills reinforcement when you have embarked upon a program of self-evaluation and decision-making for your students. They can then select both game and skills to be worked on.

Getting Started With Games

Should students select their games to play?

Guided self-selection of learning games may be most appropriate when you have developed games to meet the needs of specific students rather than those of all students in your group. Diagnostic teaching techniques as described in Chapter 3 (page 31) might also indicate specific concept or skill needs that could be reinforced by particular games that you might want to suggest as being useful to students. Your guidance should help students select games or game task cards that will help strengthen their skills. You might want to identify the concepts or skills that can be reinforced by specific games or game task cards as you acquire new games or task card sets. You may introduce particular game or task card sets when you move into various units or introduce new skills or concepts to be developed.

You might have a Games Chart on which you list games and task card sets by skill areas:

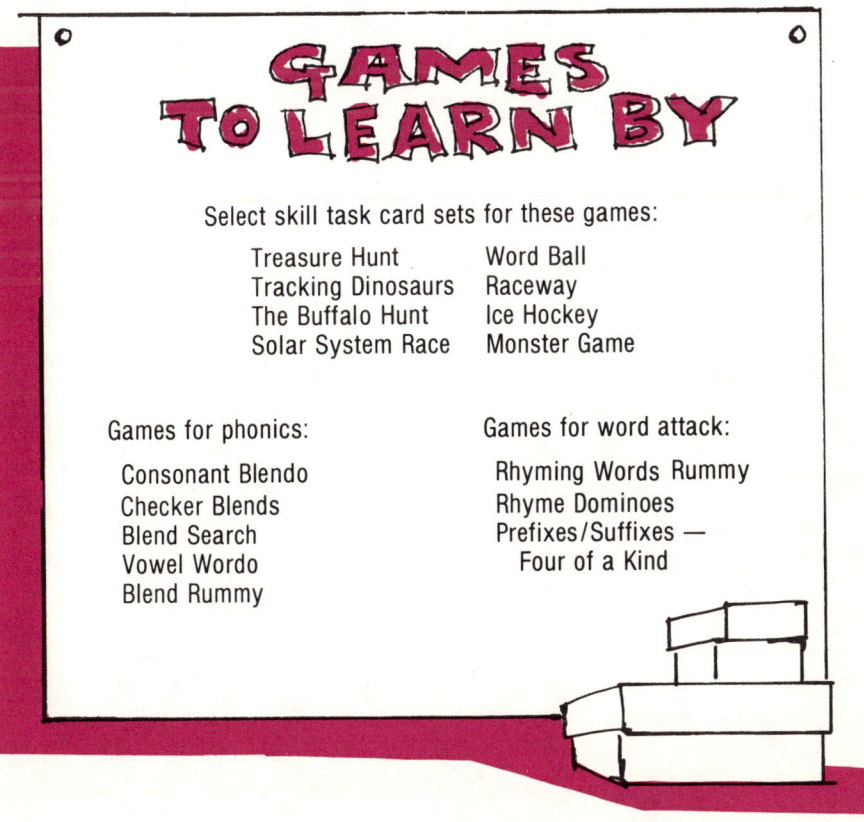

Games To Learn By

Select skill task card sets for these games:

Treasure Hunt Word Ball
Tracking Dinosaurs Raceway
The Buffalo Hunt Ice Hockey
Solar System Race Monster Game

Games for phonics:

Consonant Blendo
Checker Blends
Blend Search
Vowel Wordo
Blend Rummy

Games for word attack:

Rhyming Words Rummy
Rhyme Dominoes
Prefixes/Suffixes —
Four of a Kind

Games As Learning Tools

You might want to use a sign-up chart for those students who will be using learning games or centers for specific periods.

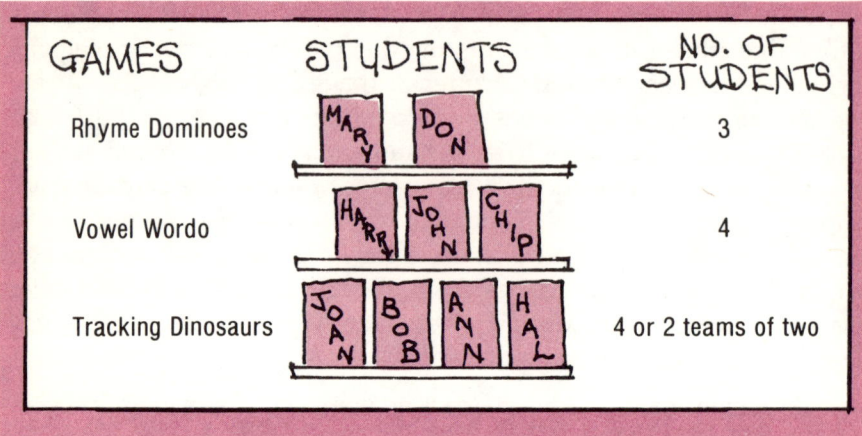

If you are using both learning games and centers and are making specific skill center assignments, you might also include listing several games that can be used to reinforce the same skills for self-selection. You might develop a chart recording not only centers but also games that can be used for specific concept or skills reinforcement:

Center/Game Objective	Center No.	Game	Game Task Card Sets
Match words and definitions	1, 4	*	III-2, etc.
Divide words into syllables	2, 3	*	II-3,
Locate information in index	5, 12	*	IV-1,
Identify affixes	10, 11	*	II-4,
			*Any game board

Getting Started With Games

Are there any special tips for organizing games for learning activities?

1. Make learning games and games parts easily accessible so students do not have to disturb other students trying to get the game to play. Storage on shelves should be ample so that game boards and game parts boxes are easily seen.
2. Packaging of games should include use of envelopes or boxes for storage of game parts so that they can be easily identified and available.
3. Arrange to have specified areas in the classroom for playing games while you are working with small groups - - particular desk areas, corner, or open-space areas.
4. Limit number of students for playing specific games. Trial and error will help you identify how many students can play different games without disturbing others.

5. Assign student helpers for checking that all games are returned intact to the storage area.

Games As Learning Tools

6. Enlist the help of parent volunteers and older student tutors to assist students while playing learning games as you are working with teacher-directed activities. It is essential that aides are given an orientation lesson as to the use of games as learning activities and how they are to supervise students playing of games.

7. Evaluate students' performance of specific concepts and skills in the games. Both teacher and student self-evaluation should be a part of organizing games for learning activities. As a result of this evaluation, you will know if a student needs more work with a given skill or concept.

8. A record keeping system that you develop appropriate to your objectives can help in planning future instructional activities. Include these key questions for students:
   - How did you like the game?
   - How could you improve the game?
   - Do you think you need more work with this skill?

There are many ways that you may use learning games. How and when learning games become a part of your curriculum depends on your unique classroom situation in terms of organization and students. It will be a matter for you to try the various ideas presented here that you think might be helpful and then choose the most effective ways you can use games as learning activities.

Chapter 3

Using Games Diagnostically

Why use games for diagnosis?
How can games be used diagnostically?

Effective teaching is based upon knowing your students. Teaching diagnostically enables you to plan learning activities geared to the needs of your particular students. Before you make instructional decisions concerning curriculum or methodology, you need information about your students' interests, learning styles, attitudes, and experiential backgrounds, as well as their specific skill strengths and skill needs. Rather than planning more generalized activities that may be too easy for some students and too advanced for others, you are able to provide a varied amount of reinforcement activities as necessary. Games provide an educational source which can be tapped successfully for specific information about your students' mastery of concepts and skills.

There are many ways to obtain information about students. The term, *diagnosis,* has been used to designate means of identifying student skill strengths and needs. Traditionally it has been assumed that diagnosis belonged in the domain of highly trained specialists such as psychologists and those who work with reading and learning disabilities. Within this framework, students referred to these specialists by their classroom teachers would be assessed through an assortment of diagnostic procedures. The results of this type of diagnosis would usually be analyzed and interpreted by the appropriate specialist. Often, however, little assistance in actual instructional modification would be provided to the classroom teacher.

Increasingly, classroom teachers are taking an active part in the diagnostic sequence. In this more informal approach, diagnostic insights can be obtained prior to and/or following instruction. For example, prior

Games As Learning Tools

to a lesson on key geography concepts and vocabulary, the teacher might pre-check student knowledge in a variety of ways, such as through games, closure fill-in-the-blank activities, or every-pupil-response activities. The lesson will then be conducted according to the skill strengths of individual students. In a diagnostic teaching situation, the teacher is continually making instructional decisions based upon such informal diagnosis of students.

Why use games for diagnosis?

Classroom games are especially well-suited for informal diagnosis. First, the gaming format considerably lessens the student apprehension which often accompanies test-taking. The "fear of testing" has been recognized by clinic authorities as adversely affecting the performance of many students in a diagnostic setting. Therefore, much time is spent and emphasis is placed on establishing rapport with children prior to actual testing in these more formal diagnostic sessions. With games, however, this fear factor is negligible as children become **involved** in the activity. Additionally, students tend to see games as **fun** expreiences. As non-school activities, students become quickly involved and tend to ignore distractions, such as an observer, in the game environment. Sullivan and Humphrey (1973) discuss the value of using games diagnostically, and extend this view to include the importance of communicating skill mastery to the student through game successes. Specifically, they confirm that the use of games:

> ... appears to act as a means for releasing the emotional blockage that inhibits any attempt to perform the intellectual reading tasks involved. And once these children participate successfully in such activities, ... the process of building more positive attitudes toward reading and a feeling that they can learn is begun. Needless to say, once the teacher has observed a higher-level performance of children in this setting it is important ... to recognize that they were able, and did, perform the skill involved. Such children need to be shown they *can* and *have* mastered a skill with specific evidence that they have learned.

"From Sullivan, Dorothy D. and James H. Humphrey, TEACHING READING THROUGH MOTOR LEARNING, 1973. Courtesy of Charles C Thomas, Publisher, Springfield, Illinois."

Using Games Diagnostically

Another facet of gaming which makes it especially appropriate for informal diagnosis is that, unlike formal testing, games can be developed which correlate closely with curriculum. These games can be very specific in regard to skills, and therefore can be especially helpful in targeted areas of individual teacher concern. For example, in the *Match the Sound* game, described on page 123, the teacher has carefully selected specific blends for the student to identify in the beginnings of words, appropriate to the current instructional plan. As students become more involved in this game, the teacher as observer can quickly and easily tell which students' responses to game tasks come easily and are correct. In addition to providing the teacher with important information about student performance in specific skills, games can help to identify other important aspects of student ability. Much individual variation in learning styles can be picked up as students interact with each other, relate to game task requirements, and respond to challenges. Some children will be impulsive in behavior; others will take their time and think through problem situations carefully. Some will require much structuring of the task, while others will grasp the game procedures quickly and clearly (Davey, 1976).

A final strength of the gaming format for diagnosis lies in ease of collecting information. Whereas formal testing can require much time and some knowledge of test administration, games can be used easily, quickly, and whenever they can "fit into" instructional situations without being disrupted by curricular objectives.

How can games be used diagnostically?

Games can be valuable adjuncts to a diagnostic program, and can be used in at least three ways:
1. by informal observation of student performance in classroom games
2. by use of a specific game to meet a diagnostic objective
3. by adjustment of a formal test into a gaming format

The most informal use of games would be teacher observation of students in a gaming situation. This approach often results in an immediate instructional adjustment, as information is collected about an individual student's strengths and needs.

Games As Learning Tools

For example, in the *Rhyme Chase* game described on page 104, the teacher may observe the following responses:

Mary: responded quickly and correctly.

> **Hypotheses**: Mary probably understands the concept of rhyming words, possesses necessary auditory perceptual skills, and can read and rhyme her vocabulary terms.

Mark: responded slowly and incorrectly whenever his turn came.

> **Hypotheses**: Mark may not understand the concept of rhyming words; he may not have the necessary auditory perceptual skills, and/or he may not be able to read his vocabulary terms.

The teacher-diagnostician could make some immediate instructional decisions. Mary might be encouraged to proceed in her sequential reading program; Mark might receive additional assistance in word rhyming from his teacher or fellow student before proceeding. Also, Mark's teacher might initiate additional diagnosis to test the initial hypotheses.

A second application of game-use for diagnosis occurs when you select a specific game to meet a diagnostic objective. In this case, you carefully match specific students with an appropriate game, observe

Using Games Diagnostically

performances, and record responses. For example, a classroom teacher might consider these three steps:

Step One: Formulate a diagnostic question.
Do Mark and Mary know their addition and subtraction facts?

Step Two: Select an appropriate game.
. . . *Math Rummy* (see page 110)

Step Three: Record observations
Mark: appears to know all addition facts presented, appears not to know the following subtraction facts: 15-9, 14-9, 23-8.

Mary: appears to know all the addition and subtraction facts presented.

In this more formalized approach to diagnosis, classroom instructional adjustment may result immediately, and/or further diagnosis may be initiated.

A third strategy for using games diagnostically involves adapting an existing "test" into a game format. We have found this to be a successful adjustment for highly anxious students evaluated at the University of Maryland Reading Clinic. Again, students' performance levels will tend to be higher when they can "lose themselves" in a non-threatening game situation. A specific example of this type of adaptation would include printing (or typing) items from a word recognition test onto attractive cards, and playing a simple game where the student calls out the words as he or she draws the cards. Although it might not be appropriate to compute the student's score according to standard test guidelines, the diagnostician can use the information to identify patterns of skill strengths and needs.

What special considerations should you keep in mind when using games diagnostically?

To maximize the effectiveness of games for diagnosis, the following three suggestions should be carefully considered:

1. Have a clear understanding of the game, both from the standpoint of skill objective and from the standpoint of the learning styles involved.
2. Keep careful records of the behaviors observed.
3. Encourage student self-evaluation.

Games As Learning Tools

The importance of a clear understanding of the skill or concept being tested in the diagnostic game cannot be overemphasized. Look carefully at the specific skills or concepts required for the activity:

Do they reflect the intended objective?
What additional skills do the students need to bring to the activity?
What modalities are involved?

For example, in the *Rhyme Chase* game described on page 104, you might evaluate the activity in the following manner, using a 3 x 5 file card:

File Card Evaluation:

Game Title: *Rhyme Chase* Game Format: *active circle*
Major Skill/Concept: *Rhyming Words*
Additional Skills: *1. Concept of rhyming; 2. Ability to read words; 3. Need auditory perceptual skills; 4. Following directions*
Modalities: *Auditory, large muscle movement*

Extending this game evaluation further, you might consider additional questions. These questions should be considered in this skills-diagnosis setting as well as in a developmental learning program in which games are used as reinforcers of skills:

What is the level of interpersonal interaction required?
Is response time a critical factor in the activity?
Is the game going to match with student interest?

Unless games are evaluated carefully, a real danger exists that student responses could be difficult to interpret. A student who is a slow, careful responder may be inappropriately labeled as deficient in identifying and categorizing science-unit vocabulary as a result of his or her poor performance on *Category Rummy* (page 105), a game which requires *speed* in reaction time as well as *skill* mastery. Likewise, a student who is unsuccessful in *Seven-Card Up* (page 127) may be

Using Games Diagnostically

demonstrating an inability to blend sounds together (the objective of the game), *or* the player may be demonstrating difficulties in any one of a number of other task requirements, from visual discrimination of individual letters (can he or she tell them apart?) to the sound-symbol relationship of individual letters (can the student "sound them out"?).

For game diagnosis to be successful, an effective and efficient system of **record keeping** is required. Several strategies have been used successfully by classroom teachers. Three of these are discussed in the next few paragraphs.

1. Develop card files on selected students. Cards should be dated and the diagnostic observation recorded. Over a short period of time, performance **patterns** will be identifiable, from which instructional adjustments can be planned.

    Student Performance Card:

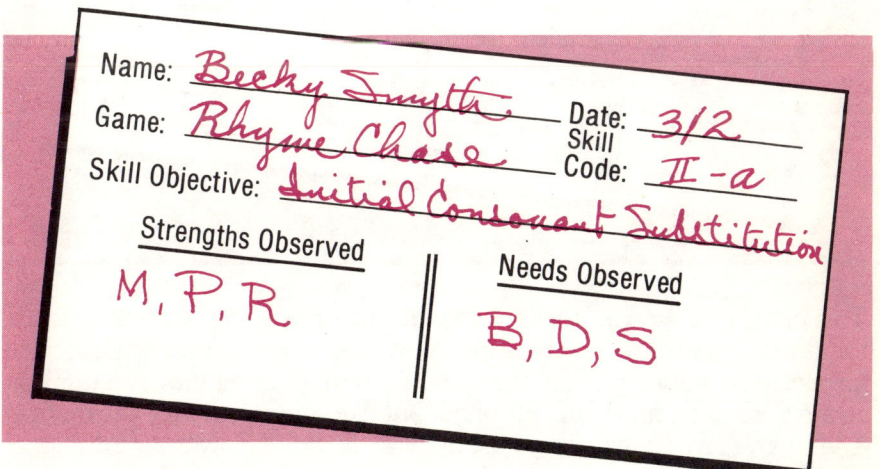

2. Develop a charting strategy for individual students and/or groups of students. This chart or checklist may include diagnostic information from other sources in addition to game performance. On the sample

Games As Learning Tools

chart illustrated below you can indicate skill mastery (+) or skill instruction needed (✓) for specific students in the area of word analysis. The information is obtained from student performance on games (G), learning centers (LC), worksheets (W), and in context (Con).

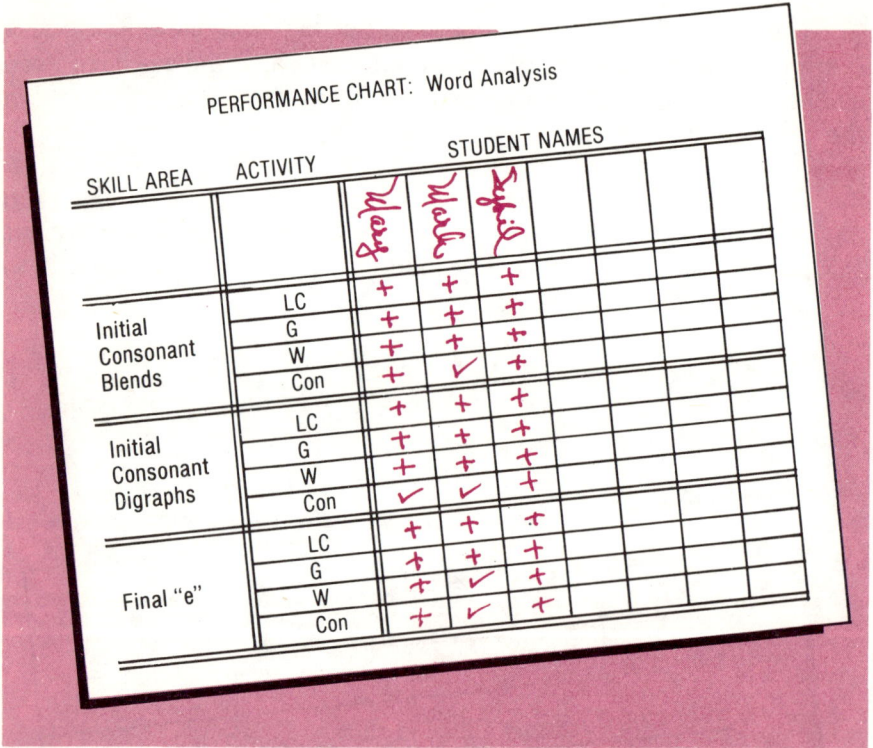

This chart enables you to identify patterns of skill strengths and needs for students, and it suggests appropriate classroom grouping strategies for skills development. For example, both Mary and Mark can demonstrate understanding of initial consonant digraphs when they see them in a learning center, game, or worksheet format. However, additional practice is necessary in situations requiring contextual application. These two students may profit from a teamed activity in which they are challenged to locate words with initial consonant digraphs from their language experience stories or from their books. Further learning activities then could include learning centers and games that call for identification of consonant digraph words from basal readers, library books, or cereal boxes.

Using Games Diagnostically

3. You might also find it helpful to record information about students on individual charts. Your chart might be as informal as this:

Student Name: Mary			
SKILL	TYPE OF ACTIVITY	DATE	RATING
Science Unit Vocabulary (Weather)	Game: Category Rummy	Feb. 11	responses were direct
'Weather' vocabulary usage	Written report on Weather reports in newspapers	Feb. 15	needs addit. help in spelling

Finally, students should be encouraged to self-evaluate their performance on the game tasks. You may wish to provide them with a checklist or checkcard to guide their evaluation, which you would then use in the instructional planning and conferencing.

A sample checkcard:

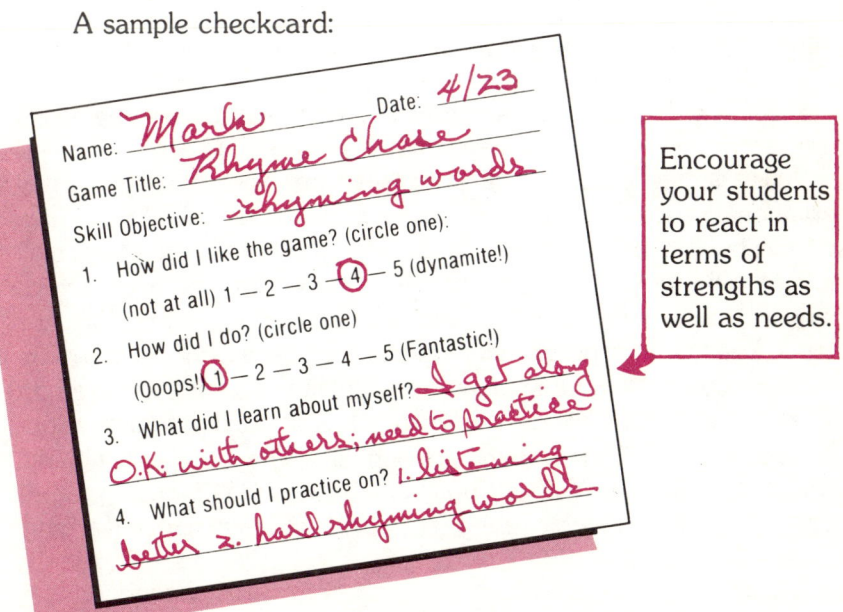

Name: Marla Date: 4/23
Game Title: Rhyme Chase
Skill Objective: rhyming words

1. How did I like the game? (circle one):
   (not at all) 1 — 2 — 3 —④— 5 (dynamite!)
2. How did I do? (circle one)
   (Ooops!)①— 2 — 3 — 4 — 5 (Fantastic!)
3. What did I learn about myself? I get along O.K. with others; need to practice
4. What should I practice on? 1. listening better 2. hard rhyming words

> Encourage your students to react in terms of strengths as well as needs.

Games As Learning Tools

A sample checklist:

GAME	My Name: Mary																		
	Date 3/21					Date 3/24					Date 3/28					Date				
	1	2	3	4	5	1	2	3	4	5	1	2	3	4	5				
Story Rummy SKILL: VOCABULARY *definitions science*			✓					✓					✓						
Category Rummy SKILL: VOCABULARY *Weather*	✓						✓						✓						

Numbers represent skill self-evaluation rating. 1 = low   5 = high

In conclusion, games offer opportunities for obtaining important diagnostic information about students in classrooms or clinical settings. The game format is uniquely appropriate for identifying skill performance levels of highly anxious students. Additionally, it can be easily incorporated into an existing instructional program. There are several ways to use games for diagnostic purposes, varying from very informal observational procedures to more formal approaches. With these diagnostic teaching approaches you need to keep in mind concept or skill objectives, a method of student self-evaluation, and a system of record-keeping as you proceed to select and develop learning games for your students. Evaluation of performance of learning tasks with games results not in assigning grades but in planning for further instruction based on students' strengths and needs. There are many possibilities for developing a stimulating and fun learning atmosphere. The word is creativity. The next three chapters will help you launch your ideas for using games both diagnostically and for learning. You're on your own. Good learning!

Chapter 4

Designing and Making Games

Where do I get ideas for designing learning games?
How can I make games attractive enough to appeal to students?
How do I adapt commercial games for skills reinforcement?

Where do I start?

While there are a number of games on the market designed for concept and skills reinforcement, particularly in the reading and math areas, budget limitations of school systems make it necessary for teachers to use their own resources in developing games. Such teacher-made games actually can provide more meaningful learning activities since the games are designed within the context of the specific group's own needs and experience background. Games can:

1. Focus on the abilities of the students of your specific group.
   For example:
   Basic game whose format and theme appeals to older students can utilize concept and skill task cards reflecting specific needs of the severely disabled learner.
2. Utilize your students' particular interests.
   For example:
   - Game boards laid out as ice-hockey arena, football or soccer fields, or a basketball court with appropriate rules have special appeal for the middle-grade students and above.
   - Game boards with Charlie Brown and Raggedy Ann themes have more appeal to primary grade students.
   - Monsters, pirates, and spacemen themes appeal to the intermediate grade students.

Games As Learning Tools

3. Reflect units of study in other curriculum areas.
   For example:
   - A board game, *Tracking Dinosaurs,* (see page 49), reflecting an intermediate grade science unit, can be used with different subject area game task cards that reinforce the week's spelling words, a language arts lesson on punctuation, or a word analysis skill for reading. The game board utilizes pictures and names of dinosaurs and thereby also reinforces the particular unit concepts and vocabulary as well as the other skills.
   - A board game, *Plains Indians Buffalo Hunt,* reflects an intermediate grade unit in social studies, similarly can be used to reinforce other subject area concepts and skills by the game task cards used. The game board reinforces concepts about the Plains Indians' dress, shelter, food, and hunting procedures by the pictures used on the game board.

The concerns of costs and time involved in constructing games, however, must be considered and met. It is essential that school systems' budgets begin to provide sufficient funding for teacher-made instructional materials such as games. Materials for games contruction can be purchased more economically by systems than by individual teachers. PTA groups and other parent-school groups may be interested in supporting these areas until the school budget allocations become adequate.

Designing and constructing learning games is far simpler than many teachers imagine. Teachers who have attended games construction workshops find that the whole notion of making their own learning games is entirely feasible. These teachers find that not only can they reproduce games from ones they've seen, but also that they themselves can design their own interesting games. The ideas for designing and constructing games presented here are not just our own. We are passing along many ideas teachers have shared with us.

Designing and Making Games

Where do I start in developing learning games?

1. First you will want to identify skills and concepts that *all* students will need opportunities to practice and apply in the subject areas for which you are responsible. In reading, you can design games to reinforce sight vocabulary, word analysis skills, comprehension, and study-reference skills. In language arts, learning games can reinforce spelling, punctuation usage, capitalization, vocabulary meaning, and syntactic language elements. In math, games can help to develop and reinforce concepts and skills in the number systems, processes, measurement, the monetary system, as well as vocabulary, and its graphic system. In science and social studies concepts, vocabulary, and skills can be developed in each unit area. Curriculum guides can be helpful in identifying concepts and skills.

Teachers we have worked with have reported favorably about working in teams to identify these concepts and skills. Some of the teams have been from one grade level. Other teams have been teachers from several grade levels working together in an open-space area. Secondary-level teams are most often teachers from one department. One particular school concerned with severely disabled readers used interdisciplinary teams of ninth and tenth grade teachers for such an activity in order to see if learning games, centers, and other activities could be developed to reinforce several subject areas simultaneously.

2. Next, you will need to become familiar with the various types of games that could be utilized. The following list summarizes the most basic types of games that have been adapted successfully for learning games:

Passive Games	Active Games
card games	relay races
Bingo-type	circle games
concentration	tag games
checkers	stunt games
dominoes	(pitching, tossing)
board games	
crossword puzzles	
paper-pencil type (scrambled words, etc.)	

Games As Learning Tools

3. Familiarize yourself with the manner in which games can be adapted as learning games. Each of these games might be adapted to the interests of the students, the focus of the curriculum in the content areas both in respect to concepts and skills, and the needs of the students. The following list shows how various games can be adapted to concept and skills reinforcement at different grade levels. The first example is the game of checkers that has been adapted as a learning game[1].

Game Parts: 2 sets of checkers — enough black and red checkers to cover all squares
                1 set of task cards with the same pictures as those fastened on the squares on the checker board. The task cards are placed face down in a pile.

Procedures: a. Choose players (two players or a buddy team) to represent each color.
                b. Players select a color of checkers.
                c. Players toss a coin to see who begins the game.
                d. The first player draws a card from the task card pile. If the student has the same picture on his or her side of the board, that player places one of his or her checkers on that square and keeps the task card. If the player does not have the same picture on his or her side of the board as the one on the task card that was drawn, the player returns the task card to the bottom of the pile.
                e. The other players then proceed in the same manner.
                f. The player who covers his or her side of the board first, wins.

Using this basic procedure for game play, checkers can be utilized to reinforce numerous concepts and skills. Types of concepts and skills at the various grade levels that could be used include:

CHECKERS

Readiness Level	Board	Task Cards
	colors	colors
	numerals	numerals
	shapes	shapes
	letters	letters

[1]Game adapted for severely disabled readers in the University of Maryland Reading Clinic by Ogden Denellen and Deanne Poole.

Designing and Making Games

	Board	Task Cards
Primary Level	colors	words for colors
	numerals	words for numerals
	number of objects	words for number objects
	shapes	words for shapes
	words	words (visual match)
Intermediate Level	root words	words with affixes
	words	synonyms
	words	antonyms
	words	dictionary phonetic respelling
	map symbols	symbols or definitions
Middle and High School Level	vocabulary of subject-area units	definitions
	math symbols	words
	formulas	processes

Another example of a basic game that can be adapted to various grade level skills and concept reinforcement is the game of *Concentration*. For those not familiar with the game, it is played by placing a number of paired cards at random face down on the floor, desk, or game board. The number of pairs can vary. Each player takes a turn turning up two cards. If the player turns up a matched pair, he or she scores a point and that pair of cards is removed. If the player does not turn up a matched pair, both cards are replaced face down. The next player proceeds in like manner. The play continues until all pairs are matched. The person with the highest score wins. This game can be adapted to various grade levels.

CONCENTRATION

	Pairs of Cards
Readiness Level	objects in pictures
	numerals
	letters
Primary Level	words
	phrases
	synonyms
	antonyms

Games As Learning Tools

<u>Pairs of Cards</u>

<u>Intermediate Level</u>	subject-area vocabulary, definitions roots-affixes that could be used to make up words words-phonetic respellings
<u>Middle and High School Level</u>	subject-area vocabulary- definitions formulas- processes

DOMINOES

The traditional game of dominoes can also be adapted to the concepts and skills of various grade levels. A word of caution, however. Be sure you follow the basic domino frequency pattern so that your game will play at an appropriate pace (see page 82). Dominoes can be adapted to the following concepts and skills:

<u>Readiness Level</u>	beginning sound pictures number quantities in pictures rhyming
<u>Primary Level</u>	sight vocabulary phrases words with "ed," "ing," "s" endings
<u>Intermediate Level</u>	minimum visual discrimination words and phonetic respellings using diacritical marking root words
<u>Middle and High School Level</u>	subject-area vocabulary, definitions root words with different affixes formulas-names of processes

Theme ideas for board games should also reflect the maturity, interests, and achievements of students. Themes that have been used successfully by teachers include:

travel	mystery	dinosaurs/animals
hot rod/motorcycles	treasure hunts	monsters
famous detectives	sports	circuses
holidays	space	comic strip characters
	camping	famous literature characters

Designing and Making Games

4. Next you will need to select several games for each of the concepts and skills you have identified. For example, to develop the concept of shapes you should utilize a variety of games — a domino game, a checkers game, concentration, a bingo game, and task cards for a board game. You will also want to keep a balance of all types of games for developing skills. Some games will be limited to a specific skill such as *Vowel Bingo* and *Pair-of-Blends Rummy*. Such games are worth developing because they reinforce basic skills and have continuing usefulness. These games do have some flexibility in terms of the rules and types of tasks to be included in the play. Active games often have a great deal of adaptability in the learning tasks. Board games also have much adaptability by developing different sets of task cards to reinforce a variety of concepts and skills. All types of learning games are essential in order to provide a variety of reinforcement activities.

5. Share the workload in making games. If you have worked as a team to identify skills and concepts, you avoid duplication in designing games. Each team member should make specific games that will become part of a pool of games that can be periodically exchanged among the team every few weeks. There might necessarily need to be several duplications because of the number of students who would be using a particularly useful and popular game for reinforcing a particular skill. This duplication can be determined by need. For board games you may decide that each team member will make several games for the team pool. For development of the different task card sets for reinforcing the different concepts and skills, your team may decide to pool these or to have each team member make his or her own individual sets. Both approaches have been utilized to the satisfaction of the teachers involved.

Are there basic guidelines I should follow in designing games?

1. Every learning game should have a *chance element* that plays a significant part as to who wins. Winning should not be based solely on the player who is most successful in handling the concepts or skills being practiced in the game. The chance element serves to emphasize the fun of playing rather than to focus on the ability of the player to perform an intellectual task.
For example:
- In a checkers game described on page 75 the chance element is in the drawing of the cards by the players which may or may not have the same picture as those on their respective sides of the checker board.

Games As Learning Tools

- In card games, the card a player draws may or may not make a pair.
- On a board game, the number of spaces a player moves is determined by the die or the spinner. Furthermore, spaces on the board marked "Take another turn," "Move ahead one space," or more creative ones such as, "The Triceratops dinosaur has spotted you. Move ahead two spaces for cover," provide additional chance elements to lend excitement to the game.

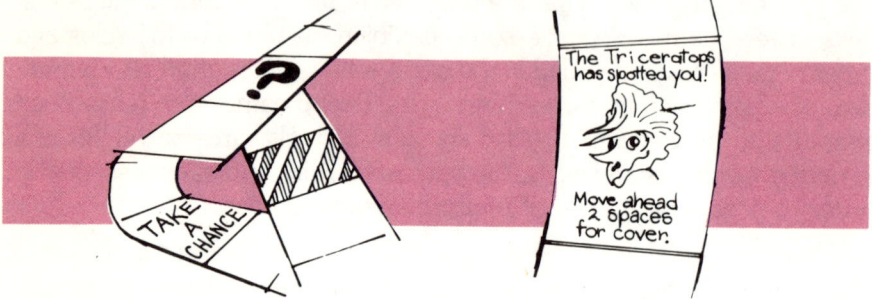

- Games can also include chance cards to be drawn whenever a double is thrown if dice are used, or if the spinner includes a chance space.
- In active games of tag the location of players may determine whether or not they are tagged by the person who is IT.
- In games requiring players to toss bean bags at a target, the spot the bean bag lands on helps to determine which list a player reads from or how many points he or she scores.
- In dominoes, the blocks each player is dealt and those which are drawn, along with the order of play, governs play.
- In concentration, the cards that are revealed by all players can help determine the success of any one player.

2. Directions for playing a game should be sequential, precise, and at a level the players can read. The age and ability level of your students will determine how simple or complex the rules of the game, and consequently its directions, will be. However, some severely disabled readers may still need someone to help them with the directions and to supervise them during the game. Teachers who have used learning games in their classrooms report that a main advantage of games is that children usually know how to play the different types. By using the basic game procedures of traditional-type games there are minimum problems

Designing and Making Games

that children encounter in following directions. However, this does not preclude making sure that directions are sequential, precise, and at a level the players can read. Rules for games should also be legibly printed and, when possible, attached to the lid of the game parts box.

An example of rules for playing a card game:

Pair of Blends Rummy

Number of players: two to four players

Directions for playing the game:

a. One player is named to serve as dealer.

b. Five cards are dealt to each player.

c. The rest of the cards are placed face down in a pile. The top card is put face side up beside the pile.

d. The player to the left of the dealer picks either the card that is face up or from the pile.

e. If the card taken from the pile makes a pair of blends with a card the player has in his or her hand, the player must lay the pair down.

f. If the player takes the face up card, he or she must play that card as a pair of blends immediately.

g. If the card drawn from the pile does not make a pair of blends, the player can keep it and discard another card from his or her hand. This discard is put face up beside the pile or this player may discard the card itself.

h. The first player to play all his or her cards and have one card left to discard calls BLENDO and ends the game.

i. Each pair of blends a player has on the board is worth five points.

j. The winner is the first player to earn ___ points. (The number of points should be determined by the desired length of the game.)

An example of directions for a board-type game:

Tracking Dinosaurs

Number of players: two to four players or two buddy teams

Game parts: spinner
markers (4)
game board
set of task cards (placed face down on the board)

Games As Learning Tools

a. Each player/team selects a marker.

b. The player/team who spins the highest number, starts.

c. The first player/team spins the spinner to find how many spaces are to be moved from the starting point.

d. Before the player/team moves a marker a task card is drawn. If the player/team completes the task correctly, that marker is moved according to the number on the spinner.

e. If a player's marker lands on a space that says "Move ahead" or "Lose a turn," the marker is moved accordingly.

f. The first player/team to finish the game, wins.

3. Use bright and varied colors for game parts, game boards, and game parts boxes.

- For game boards, poster board is recommended because it is strong enough when protected by lamination or contact-type paper and comes in a wide variety of colors. White should be used only when it sets off the illustrations to be used more effectively than if colors were used.
- Colored unlined file cards come in different sizes and can be useful for making cards for card games and game task cards.
- Light colored construction paper can also be used for game task cards, but it is not as durable.

4. Use illustrations from magazines and other printed materials for game cards and game boards if you feel that your artwork is inadequate.

- Special topic magazines that can be used for game themes are an excellent source of illustrations reflecting student interests.

Types of Magazines	Types of Illustrations
children's	story characters
nature	animals, insects, etc.
camping	camping gear, scenes
sports	all types of sports scenes
racing car	drag racing, racing cars
hot rod	funny cars, etc.
motorcycle	motorcycle scenes
travel	travel pictures
humor	zany pictures

Designing and Making Games

- Inexpensive books available in toy departments can serve as sources for illustrations for elementary grade-level games. For example, farm animals, dinosaurs, American Indians, and numerous children's characters from literature can be clipped from these books.
- Used workbooks for reading readiness are excellent sources for illustrations of beginning and ending sounds, rhyming words, long and short vowel words.
- Stickers for Charlie Brown characters, Raggedy Ann, and other characters produced by gift wrap and card companies can make interesting game boards for younger students.
- Gift wrapping paper is another source of illustrations, particularly those with cartoon characters such as Charlie Brown and Mickey Mouse.
- Publicity materials geared to children and distributed by restaurant chains can be used for game themes.
- Stylistic letters cut from advertisements are excellent for games focusing on letter recognition.
- Drivers' manuals, bike safety, and traffic law brochures include all kinds of highway signs and traffic illustrations for games such as *Highway Dominoes* and *Highway Checkers*.

5. Be creative with all types of materials for games:

Materials	Use
tin cans ice cream tubs liquor cartons potato chip cartons egg and milk cartons	for toss and pitch games

tin cans with lids
small gift boxes
plastic containers
   for margarine or
   cheese dips
	for game parts storage:
	die, markers, chance cards,
	directions for play

Games As Learning Tools

Materials	Use
ice cream tubs potato chip tubs	for fishing games
old game markers spools buttons miniature cars party favors airplanes, etc. Charlie Brown erasers small stones	for game markers
plastic floor runners oil cloth	for floor games (twister, concentration, bean bag toss, etc.)

Other sources of materials:
lumber yards for scraps of wood
seamstresses for scraps of material
grocery stores for pictures, produce containers
printers for scraps of paper (to make word cards or game task cards)
upholstery or fabric shops for felt and vinyl materials
old, discarded games with missing parts.

How can I construct games so that they will last?

When you are designing and constructing learning games, you should keep in mind the *adaptability, durability* and *storability* of the games in order to get the most use out of the time and money expended in developing them. Even new, commercial education games need to be examined for ways to make them more durable prior to putting them into classroom use.

1. Guidelines for providing ADAPTABILITY of learning games have been discussed under guidelines for designing games on page 87. They included such points as:

- Designing a game board so that it can be flexible in terms of reinforcing more than one specific skill.

- Designing a game so that it can be played with different rules.

Designing and Making Games

- Designing a game so that it can be played with each player using his or her own word bank words or set of task cards when it is that player's turn.

2. Guidelines for DURABILITY of games include:
- Avoid use of water-soluble paints, markers, or crayons unless the playing surface is covered by contact-type paper or plastic spray.
- Protect playing surface and back cover of game boards and cards with clear contact-type paper or clear plastic spray. Some clear hair sprays have been found to be suitable as well as gloss fixatives that are available through art supply stores.

- Use durable materials for game boards such as tag board or the more expensive and stiffer matting and illustration board.
- Reinforce edges and corners of game boards with Mystic-type cloth or electrician's plastic tape, both of which are available in several colors and different widths.
- Oil cloth or plastic covering material (vinyls) for table cloths and upholstery are useful materials for game boards as well as floor games.
- Plastic floor runners make durable floor mats for such games as hop scotch, concentration, or bean bag toss.

3. Guidelines for proving STORABILITY of games include:
- Provide a box or covered plastic container for game parts. Sturdy brown envelopes might be used though they are not as durable as boxes.
- Cover game board back and box for game parts with matching contact-type paper. If a game is adapted to several skill games, there may be several boxes matching the game board back but each is labeled according to its specific skill with your system of coding skills.
- If game boards are large and need to be folded, score the back of the game board where it is to be folded with the dull, back edge of a knife or scissors so that it will bend easily in a sharp line. The folded edge should then be covered with tape.

Games As Learning Tools

It has been found that a half of a regular-size poster board sheet makes an adequate size game board 14″ x 22″. This size need not be folded. It is also possible to put a game on each side of this size game board which helps to reduce significantly the cost of constructing games. Using two sides of a game board enables you to provide more games for less cost. However, you cannot increase the number of students who can play games at a given time with this method, only an additional variety of games. Additional guidelines will be presented in Chapter 5.

How can commercial games be adapted to learning games?

Many teachers have been quite resourceful in adapting commercial games to learning games.

- Board games can be played as they usually are played. But, as in teacher-made games, before a player can move, he or she must make a correct response to a game task card that reinforces a specific concept or skill. Such board games must be of the type that is basically one of moving from start to finish without a lot of elaborate procedures to be completed at each move. Games like Uncle Wiggly and Candy Land have been efficiently adapted in this way for younger students.

- Checkers game boards can be converted by attaching stickers with words or pictures to each square and played as described on page 75.

- Playing cards, such as ones designed with Charlie Brown characters, can be adapted by pasting pictures for such skills as beginning or ending sounds in words on the faces of the cards. When this is done, a new box is needed since the original card case will no longer hold the deck of cards. Plain adhesive stickers of different sizes can also be attached to these cards and then printed on the stickers.

- Some dominoes have been successfully adapted to skills practice by fastening new faces to the dominoes with different skill focus as described on page 81. However, most adaptations of dominoes are more successfully developed by using tag or illustration board weight paper to make the dominoes to which pictures are attached or on which words are printed. These are then covered with clear contact-type paper.

Designing and Making Games

- Old and battered game boards have been used as backing for new games. Teachers have applied a new game face to the old board, protected the new game board and backing with contact-type paper, and then edged the redone gameboard with tape as described on page 53.

A number of teachers have reported success in collecting old game parts by sending out requests to parents and people in the community to contribute old games to the schools. Their adaptation of old games indicates that this is another valuable source for developing learning games.

Games construction takes time. There are several sources of help upon whom the teacher may discover in an effort to develop a sufficient selection of games for a classroom. Teachers who have been using games as learning activities in their classrooms have found the following ways to get help in constructing games:

- Teams of teachers have shared in games construction after they have, as teams, identified concepts and skills that need reinforcement. They have pooled their efforts in constructing games to prevent unnecessary duplication of games and to provide students with a greater variety of games by sharing them.

- Teachers have found help in making games they have designed through teacher aides as a part of their non-instructional assignments.

- Students are also helpful in making game parts or doing the manuscript printing of words and task cards.

Games As Learning Tools

- Students have developed new rules for games. They have also created completely new games. These have been enthusiastically and effectively carried out by intermediate and middle school students.

- Parent volunteers are another source of help in games construction.

- Classroom teachers report that parent volunteers working individually or in workshops are able to develop teacher-designed materials including learning games and centers.

In all cases, the teachers found that they needed to collect the materials and provide models of the game parts to be made to assure quality control. It is of particular importance that aides and parents who have made parts of games be shown the completed game so that they can see how they contributed to the student's concepts or skills development.

Have workshops proved helpful for constructing games?

Workshops for parent volunteers have been successful for games construction. Such workshops have been originated by individual teachers or through a cooperative effort between teachers and parents. They may be 'once a year' workshops or may be scheduled on a monthly basis. Careful preplanning and organization is essential to their success. Some schools have found parents who were able to take almost complete charge of organizing such workshops. Preplanning includes collecting ample supplies and materials that will be needed for game parts construction. Models of the game parts to be made should be ready for demonstration. Samples of completed games should also be on display.

Materials needed include:
- paper, magic markers, rubber cement, rulers, pencils, scissors in sufficient quantity, contact-type papers, tape, boxes, containers, string.
- specific material to make game parts, or models for game parts.

Designing and Making Games

Parent volunteers often need some direction and guidance during the workshop. Specific direction should be provided at the beginning of the workshop to go over what needs to be done and to demonstrate any particular technique that might be needed. If an aide or teacher cannot be present during the entire workshop, arrangements should be made so that someone is available to be called on if a problem develops. At the conclusion of the workshop those teachers whose game parts have been worked on should stop in to make arrangements for the parents to see the games when they have been completed. This might be done at the next regularly scheduled workshop. The teachers in the building may want to show their appreciation to the parent volunteers by having an informal party for them at the end of the year. Other forms of recognition could include: setting up a bulletin board display citing those who contributed their help, or by sending thank-you letters or certificates to those who participated in the workshops. Public recognition of their work helps to ensure further parent-teacher partnership.

Games As Learning Tools

    Teacher workshops have also proven successful in constructing games and learning centers. Here useful idea sharing often takes place. Teachers working together can often aid each other by their suggestions for handling particular problems. It has also been found that teachers often can demonstrate new ways with construction of a game — new materials they have found, new ways to construct a game, a new idea for a game. Such workshops have been scheduled prior to the opening of school. One such workshop was even scheduled by the teachers themselves at one teacher's home over the weekend. They reported having a great time and had some excellent products to show for their unique efforts. This book itself attests to the many ideas that teachers can give to each other. As noted at the beginning of this book, the authors are indebted to many, many teachers who have shared their ideas with us as we all try to develop the most stimulating and rewarding of learning experiences for students.

Chapter 5

Formats/Directions/ And Basic Game Guidelines

What are the basic game formats?
What are the directions and specific guidelines applicable for each basic game format?
Which games should I use?

As you plan for inclusion of learning games into your instructional program, you will want to have plenty of game format ideas from which to choose. It is the objective of Chapters 5 and 6 to provide you with alternative game types and specific ideas which can be applied across content speciality areas and at various instructional levels, K-12.

This chapter will describe ten basic passive and active game formats that have been found to be most appropriate for classroom use:

Passive game formats	Active game formats
Bingo	Circle
Card Games	Relay
Checkers	Tag
Concentration	Stunt
Dominoes	
Board Games	

The descriptions of the basic game formats will include Game Directions and Game Guidelines. After each basic game format section, a summary chart appears. This chart includes specific games described in Chapter 6 utilizing that format. The games listed on each chart follow the organizational framework found in Chapter 6. Games on each basic game

Games As Learning Tools

format chart are listed according to subject area, the four content skills that cut across all subject areas, and levels of difficulty. The four content skill areas include:

<u>Vocabulary</u> — activities which develop and reinforce meaningful vocabulary in the subject areas.

<u>Concepts and Facts</u> — activities which reinforce concepts and facts in subject areas.

<u>Word Analysis</u> — activities which reinforce word attack skills, word parts, or spelling patterns for dealing with unfamiliar words in subject-area reading materials.

<u>Graphic-Symbolic Skills</u> — activities which reinforce non-verbal symbols and their meanings in the various subject areas.

The levels of difficulty include:

<u>Primary Level</u> — appropriate for students in grades K-2

<u>Intermediate Level</u> — appropriate for students in grades 3-5

<u>Middle Level</u> — appropriate for students in grades 6-8

<u>Senior Level</u> — appropriate for students in grades 9-12

How to Use this Chapter:

Descriptions of basic game formats in this chapter differ according to whether they are passive or active. The passive games include specific directions and overall guidelines for designing, constructing, and playing each particular type of game. The active games include only general guidelines for using active games leaving specific, detailed directions for these particular types of play that are usually unique for each active game to Chapter 6.

As you become involved in creating learning games you will sense the limitless possibilities for format ideas. The basic game types presented in this chapter are not intended to limit or restrict your creative involvement with games, but rather to provide you with starting point ideas from which you can develop to their greatest potential a full range of game alternatives.

- Overview this chapter for basic game formats and their variations.
- Refer back to the appropriate format sections for help as you begin to implement specific game ideas from Chapter 6 in your classroom.

Formats/Directions/And Basic Game Guidelines

- Note variations of basic game formats that would be most appropriate for developing and reinforcing content skills in your students.
- Use the charts for each basic game format as a cross-reference for providing a variety of games to develop and reinforce specific concepts and skills.

Passive Game Formats:

BINGO

Bingo Game Directions:

Each player is given a bingo card divided into spaces making vertical, horizontal, and diagonal rows. Words, numbers, or sounds are written in the spaces. A pack of task cards for the Caller and discs for the players are needed. The Caller presents the word or task, orally or visually by holding up the card from his or her pack, and the players cover the corresponding word or task on their bingo cards. The first player to complete a vertical, horizontal, or diagonal row calls "Bingo" and is declared the winner. This player also may become the Caller for the next game.

Bingo Game Guidelines:

1. Bingo cards can be constructed out of sturdy materials such as cardboard or regular sheets of paper. Heavier cardboard cards of the more permanent type should be protected with clear adhesive paper or plastic spray. Paper bingo cards can be protected by inserting them into acetate folders.

2. Instead of calling a word or task, or presenting it visually for students to match, the Caller can use a variety of stimulus material devised by you, the teacher.

    'Things' could be used. For example, hold up an object. Have students find a Spanish word to match the object on their cards.

    Pictures or diagrams might also be used. For example, point to parts of the body on a skeletal diagram. Have students match these parts with the correct labels on their cards. Or, hold up a picture of various cloud formations. Have students match the pictures with the correct terms on their cards.

Games As Learning Tools

Overhead transparencies are also useful. For example, sentences with key vocabulary words deleted are projected. Students then fill in the appropriate words on their bingo cards.

The _____ lives in dry, hot lands.

WORDO

camel	fox	stork
goose		fish
alligator	polar bear	wolf

3. You can effectively differentiate the game for students of various ability levels. This provides students with different, yet synonymous, terms to place on their bingo cards. As the Caller reads the meaning, students match it to an appropriate vocabulary term. For example,

> Caller: "Where you wear your hat"
>
> a difficult term: pate
> an easy term: head

4. The traditional bingo card contains 25 squares. There may be occasions, especially with younger students, when it would be appropriate to reduce this number. Keep in mind the objective of providing successful, interesting experiences for students and limit the options when frustration or boredom are possible. For some students nine spaces would suffice.

5. Students at the readiness level might use only vertical or horizontal rows for "Bingo." It has been found that young students have difficulty noting a diagonal completion.

6. Each bingo card square need not be filled with a different item. You may *repeat* items when this seems appropriate.

7. Answer keys need to be prepared so students can check their responses.

8. Students can make their own bingo cards. This may be especially effective as a follow-up activity. For example, to follow a lesson on "landforms" in geography, elementary students colored and cut out various landforms which the teacher had drawn on a ditto sheet. The students then pasted these landforms on their bingo cards. The teacher then read definitions of these landforms and students matched the illustrations on their cards.

Formats/Directions/And Basic Game Guidelines

Summary Chart: BINGO

LEVEL	VOCABULARY	CONCEPTS AND FACTS	WORD ANALYSIS	GRAPHIC-SYMBOLIC
PRIMARY (Grades K-2)	Lang. Arts: Match words with opposites Opposites Bingo p. 99	Science: Match names of baby animals with parent Animal Bingo p. 110	Lang. Arts: Match rhyming words Rhyme Word p. 121	Math.: Match sets with numbers Math-O p. 133
INTERMEDIATE (Grades 3-5)	Soc. Studies: Match "time-line" terms with numbers Time-Line Bingo p. 102	Soc. Studies: Match fact about state with state State-O p. 113	Lang. Arts: Match number of syllable with word called Syllable Count p. 124	Music: Match symbol with word Music Notes p. 136
MIDDLE (Grades 6-8)	Lang. Arts: Match words with definitions Clue Bingo p. 105	Soc. Studies: Match famous Americans with accomplishments Guess Who p. 116	Foreign Lang.: Match conjugation with verb form Verb Find p. 127	Lang. Arts: Match abbreviations with words Brev-O p. 138
SENIOR (Grades 9-12)	Ind. Arts: Match names of parts of car engine Auto Bingo p. 107	Lang. Arts: Match job skill description with occupation Job Hunt p. 118	Lang. Arts: Match letters with those deleted in spelling words Mystery Letter p. 129	Bus. Educ.: Match shorthand symbol with word called Symb-O p. 140

Games As Learning Tools

CARD GAMES

Several basic types of card games are presented in this section in order to provide a variety for students to use as learning games. Some of the games remain very close to the original versions while others have been adapted as they have been found to be useful in the classroom. Also included are the suggested number of players for the different games.

RUMMY
(2-6 players)

Rummy Game Directions:

With the many local variations of rummy games you may prefer to use one that your students already know and adapt it to serve as a learning game.

Each player is given a specified number of cards from a deck of approximately 52 skill task cards. That is, two players would get ten cards each, three or four players would get seven cards each, and five or six players would get six cards each. The rest of the cards would be placed face down in the center of the table. The top card is turned face up and placed beside the pack. The object of the game is to collect sets of 2, 3, or 4 matching skill cards with the winner being the first player to get rid of all the cards in his or her hand.

The first player draws one card either from the pack in the center of the table or that student may take the face-up card of the discard pile. Any sets the player has in his or her hand are placed face up on the table. The player must then discard one card from his or her hand and place it face up on the discard pile. The next player may draw a card from the pack or take the top discard. Any matching sets this player has in his or her hand are placed face up on the table; this player may also add to his or her opponents' sets. The second player then discards and play continues. The first player who puts down all his or her cards is the winner.

Variations of Rummy:
- cards may be sequenced in some order.
- primary-level students match only two instead of four cards.

Formats/Directions/And Basic Game Guidelines

- *Syllabico* is a variation of rummy. Each card in the pack has one syllable or a one syllable word on it. The object of the game is to make words by putting the syllables together and placing the words face up on the table. Any player may add to another player's word until there are no possible additions. The player who makes the final addition gets to keep the word.

For example, player number one makes | bliss | + | ful |

Player number two might then add | bliss | + | ful | + | ly |

The player who uses all of his or her cards first is the winner and earns ten points. Each player then totals the number of cards in the words he or she possesses and adds these points to his or her own score. The number of total points for declaring the winner depends on the number of players or the length of the game.

MATCH

(2 players)

Match Game Directions:

All of the cards are dealt between two players. These cards contain skill tasks or words. The cards are dealt face down and are not looked at. The dealer places his or her first card face up on the table. The other player turns his or her first card face up. If the cards match according to the skill being reinforced, the first person to call "match" wins the cards, provided he or she can correctly identify the match by giving another example. For instance, if the cards that match are "tree" and "train," the player who called "match" must be able to read both words and give another word that begins with "tr." When all the cards in the players' hands have been used, those cards remaining in the center are reshuffled and redealt. The game continues until all cards are won by one player or within a time limit. Categories are selected before hand or the players determine categories as they play. In the latter case, more advanced students determine in what way matching cards are the same. Such matches might be: two words that are the same parts of speech; two words that have to do with parts of animals; words that rhyme; words that contain silent letters, etc.

Examples of categories:
    same beginning sounds   English and foreign words with same meaning
    like properties of chemicals   mathematical relationships

Games As Learning Tools

SEVEN CARD UP

(2-4 players)

Seven Card Up Game Directions:

The object of the game is to build words using the task cards. Each task card has a letter, syllable, root word, blend or digraph, or affix. Seven task cards are placed face up in the center of the table. Seven task cards are then dealt to each player. The remaining cards are put in a pile face down on the table. In turn each player draws a card from the pile and then adds as many cards as possible to <u>one</u> of the cards on the table. Play is continued until all the cards have been used or no further combinations can be made. The winner is the player with the fewest cards in his or her hand.

For example,

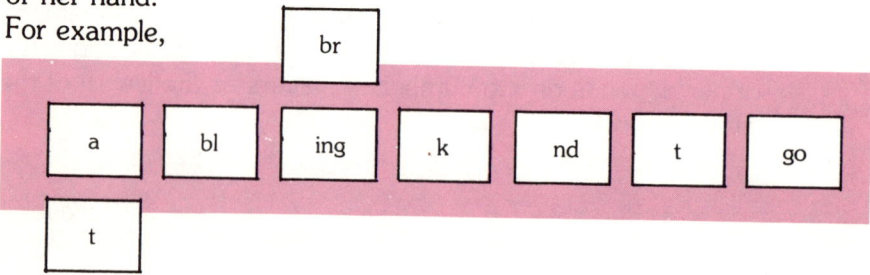

The first player draws a card from the pile on the table and makes the word <u>bring</u>. This player places one card from his or her hand on the discard pile. The next player draws and adds [t] to make the word <u>at</u>. The third player draws and then makes the word <u>flats</u> by adding [fl] and [s] to <u>at</u>; he or she then discards. Each player adds as many cards to one word as he or she wishes during his or her turn. Play continues in this manner until all cards have been used or no further combinations can be made. The winner is the player with the fewest cards in his or her hand.

Variations:
- sequencing of numbers or the alphabet
- building sentences with words
- numbers could be added, subtracted, multiplied, or divided.

POKER: SEVEN-CARD STUD

(2-7 players)

Poker Game Directions:

The object of the game is to collect some category of related cards according to the skill being reinforced. The winner is the player holding

Formats/Directions/And Basic Game Guidelines

the best 'hand'. Categories might include: parts of speech (nouns, verbs, adjectives), multi-syllable words, or vocabulary meaning with words relating to one topic (snow, rain, hail, sleet, fog). The traditional ranking of poker hands that can be adapted according to the skill being reinforced is listed in order from highest to lowest:

1. <u>Straight flush</u> — five cards in sequence, (king, queen, jack, ten, nine) or five of a kind when appropriate.
2. <u>Four of a kind</u> — four cards of one kind. (four kings or four tens)
3. <u>Full house</u> — three cards of one kind and a pair. (three kings plus two tens)
4. <u>A flush</u> — when appropriate, five cards of the same suit. (five diamonds any value)
5. <u>A straight</u> — when appropriate, any five cards in sequence but not of the same suit.
6. <u>Three of a kind</u> — three cards of one kind. (three queens)
7. <u>Two pairs</u> — two pairs of cards. (two tens plus two threes)
8. <u>One pair</u> — two cards of one kind. (two threes)

For example, in a game using multi-syllable words the following categories might be utilized:

1. Straight flush — a sequence of a five-syllable, four-syllable, <u>(40 points)</u> three-syllable, two-syllable, and a one-syllable word or five nouns.
2. Four of a kind — 4 three-syllable words, would be higher than 4 <u>(35 points)</u> one-syllable words.
3. Full house — 3 five-syllable words, pair of two-syllable words. <u>(30 points)</u>
4. A flush — 5 four-syllable words, would be higher than 5 two- <u>(25 points)</u> syllable words.
5. A straight — four words can be put into a complete sentence <u>(20 points)</u> with no regard for the number of syllables.
6. Three of a kind — 3 four-syllable words, would be higher than 3 <u>(15 points)</u> one-syllable words.

Games As Learning Tools

7. Two pairs — 2 five-syllable words and 2 one-syllable words. (10 points)
8. One pair — 2 four-syllable words, would be higher than 2 one-syllable words. (5 points)

When playing Seven-Card Stud as poker, the game takes on the dimension of betting as to which player holds the best hand. Beans or bottle caps might be used for betting purposes, with the winner holding the largest 'pot' at the end of the game. The pot may be won when every player has had the opportunity to bet, after which the hands are displayed in a 'showdown' with the best hand being given the 'pot.'

To play the game, two cards are dealt face down and one card face up to each player. Players look at their three cards and determine what they are going to attempt to collect. Players then put down an initial bet or 'ante' on the cards they have. All bets made by the players go into the 'pot' in the center of the table. After the first bet, one card is dealt face up to each player three times. After each deal there is another round of bets until each 'active' player has four cards face up on the table. To remain 'active', or to continue as a player in the game, at each round of dealing, a player must equal the highest bet placed in the pot by any one player. A last card is dealt face down to each 'active' player and there is a final bet as to whose hand is highest. After the final betting, there is the 'showdown' with each player selecting which five cards he or she will show for his or her poker hand. The winner with the highest ranking hand takes the 'pot' if the skill tasks of the five cards can be indentified correctly.

When betting is not considered advisable, the students can simply have their cards dealt to them and then they can guess what each player is trying to collect. Varying numbers of points can be assigned to the winner according to the ranking of his or her hand. A scorecard can be made to establish the ranking depending on the skills being reinforced. A player gets his or her score only if that player also identifies the skill tasks on his or her cards. Players' scores are then used to determine the overall winner of the game.

Formats/Directions/And Basic Game Guidelines

PHRASE MATCH

(3-4 players)

Phrase Match Game Directions:

This game requires a minimum of three persons. The object of the game is to build complete sentences using task cards with phrases on them. All cards are dealt to the players (approximately 10 to 12 cards each). One player is designated as the Caller. The Caller holds his or her cards with the remaining players placing their cards face up on the table. The Caller then reads a phrase orally from one of the cards in his or her hand and places it face up on the table.

Taking turns, the first person to read a complete sentence by using a phrase card from his or her own hand and the Caller's phrase keeps both cards. Phrases can be added to either end on the Caller's phrase. For example,

Caller reads	after school	
Player matches	I played	
Player reads	"I played after school."	

Phrases might be taken from students' readers or language experience stories. The winner is the player with the most cards at the end. A new Caller is designated for each game.

Variations using math skills might include:

Caller reads	4 6	"four - six"	
Player matches:			
multiplication facts		24	4 x 6
cardinal numbers*		<	4 < 6

*Players may not rearrange numbers

GO FISH

(2-4 players)

Go Fish Game Directions:

The object of *Go Fish* is to collect sets of four matching skill cards, with the winner being the first player to use all his or her cards first.

Games As Learning Tools

Seven cards are dealt to each player if two are playing, and five cards if there are more than two players. Place the rest of the pack face down.

One player says to another, "Give me all your _____." If the player has what is asked, he or she must give them up; if not he or she says, "Go Fish." The asking player then goes to the pack and takes the top card. If the top card matches what he or she is looking for, that player puts it in his or her hand and takes another turn. If the asking player gets a card he or she is asking for from another player, he or she continues to ask any player for whatever that player is trying to collect. This player stops when he or she does not get what he or she is asking either from another player or by not drawing one from the pile. The next player continues in the same manner. When a player collects four cards that match, this book is placed on the table. The winner is the first player to get rid of his or her cards.

LE BAG

(3-4 at middle or senior level)

Le Bag Game Directions:

The object of this game is to match pairs and not to get caught "Holding the bag." For older students, *Le Bag's* skill-card deck should include 24 matching pairs and three Le Bag cards. This can be adapted for younger students by using fewer cards with about twenty-five cards (11 matching pairs and three Le Bag cards). The Le Bag cards should have either the words Le Bag or a picture of a bag on them. The matching pairs of skill cards have similar characteristics according to the skill being reinforced. For example, two "br" blends, two long "a" vowel words, two four-syllable words, or two words that are synonyms or antonyms.

All the cards are dealt to the players. Each player discards all pairs of cards face up on the board. After the initial discard each player in turn shuffles his or her hand. Each player then draws a card from the hand of the person to the right. After each 'drawing' the players again put down any pairs. This procedure continues until all pairs have been matched. Since there are three Le Bag cards in the deck, only one pair can be made and one person must be left holding the 'odd' card and becomes "Le Bag."

Formats/Directions/And Basic Game Guidelines

Card Game Guidelines:

1. Often students can make their own card games. Standard three by five file cards make excellent decks of cards. It is advisable to protect the cards with clear adhesive paper or plastic spray since they must slide off each other as they are dealt. Gloss fixative does the same job as plastic spray and is particularly good when pictures or labels have not been pasted on the cards.

2. Cards approximately the size of a standard deck of cards can be purchased from printers or suppliers of paper for printers.

3. For poker games you may wish to make blank cards that have playing card suits and values so that a game can be played and scored in a traditional manner. To do this you can make a ditto master to reproduce cards on oaktag paper. For example,

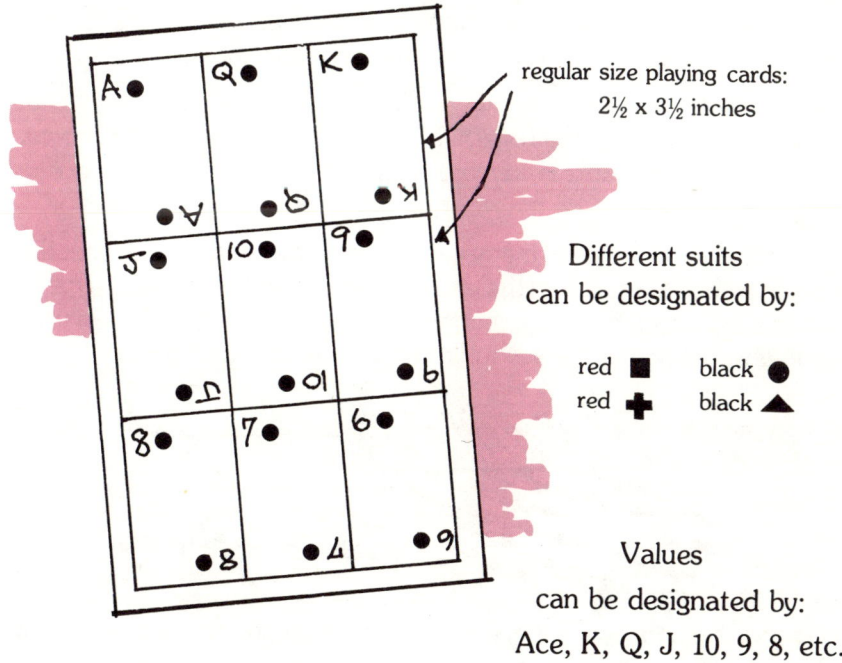

regular size playing cards:
2½ x 3½ inches

Different suits
can be designated by:

red ■   black ●
red ✚   black ▲

Values
can be designated by:
Ace, K, Q, J, 10, 9, 8, etc.

Skill tasks are printed on the cards *after* the sheets have been run off and *before* the sheets are protected by laminating or clear adhesive paper and cut into individual cards.

Games As Learning Tools

4. Regular playing cards can also be utilized for poker games by attaching adhesive labels of an appropriate size for the tasks to be reinforced. For example,

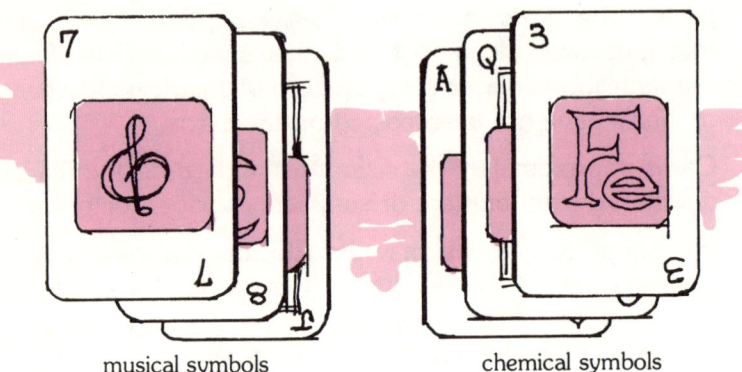

        musical symbols   chemical symbols

5. Decks for younger students should contain fewer cards. It may be necessary to amend rules slightly and have them match pairs instead of four of a kind as in Rummy, for example.

6. Many games lend themselves to "buddy" play. That is, a pair of students play one hand together. *Phrase Match, Match, Syllabico, Seven Card Up,* and *Poker* are games in which "buddy" play can help.

7. Because of the length of many games it may be necessary to time the game rather than play to the end. It is also essential not to let a game drag while waiting for a person to make a play. In this case a simple cooking timer may be set to limit the time for each play.

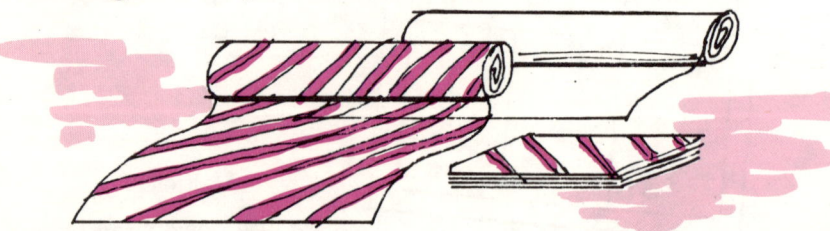

8. Decorative adhesive papers make good protective backings for skill cards with the clear adhesive paper covering the face of the cards. The same decorative design should be used for any one set of skill cards. Decorative themes should be appropriate to different age levels. The plain-color decorative adhesive makes decks of skill cards appropriate for all age levels.

Formats/Directions/And Basic Game Guidelines

Summary Chart: CARD GAMES

LEVEL	VOCABULARY	CONCEPTS AND FACTS	WORD ANALYSIS	GRAPHIC-SYMBOLIC
PRIMARY (Grades K-2)	Lang. Arts: Match colors and words <u>Color Match</u> p. 99	Math.: Pair cards with equivalent facts <u>Math Rummy</u> p. 110	Lang. Arts: Categorize pictures or words by phonic elements <u>Phonic Fish</u> p. 121	Lang. Arts: Pair upper and lower case letters <u>Alphabet Rummy</u> p. 133
INTERMEDIATE (Grades 3-5)	Lang. Arts: Match phrases to complete sentences <u>Phrase Match</u> p. 102	Lang. Arts: Sequence sentences to tell a story <u>Sentence Rummy</u> p. 113	Lang. Arts: Make words from syllable cards <u>Syllabico</u> p. 124	Math.: Pair measurement quantities <u>Measure Rummy</u> p. 136
MIDDLE (Grades 6-8)	Science: Categorize botany or weather terms <u>Category Rummy</u> p. 105	Foreign Lang.: Pair equivalent terms (synonyms) <u>Le Bag</u> p. 116	Lang. Arts: Form words from letter/letter combination cards <u>Seven Card Up</u> p. 127	Science: Categorize growth sequences of plants/animals <u>Cycle Rummy</u> p. 139
SENIOR (Grades 9-12)	Am. Hist.: Categorize history concept cards <u>History Poker</u> p. 107	Art: Categorize artists by schools (Go Fish) <u>Know Your Art</u> p. 118	Any Content Area: Form words from syllable cards <u>Syllabico</u> p. 129	Lang. Arts: Match newspaper want-ad abbreviations with words <u>Ad Match or Le Bag</u> p. 141

Games As Learning Tools

CHECKERS

Checkers Game Directions:

(Type I: Standard Checker Format)

This game is played using standard checker rules. Checkers are placed on the red spaces on the board leaving the two center rows blank. Players take turns moving diagonally into each other's territory.

A player moves one space or jumps the opponent's checker after completing a skill task. The checker the player jumps then becomes his or her's and can be used to crown a king. King checkers are crowned when a player reaches the last row of the opponent's side. King checkers can then move and jump *either* forward or backward. The game is won by capturing all the opponent's checkers.

(Type II: See page 44)

Checkers Game Guidelines:

1. Consider making board and checkers as *reusable* as possible:

Tape words onto checkers. These can then be replaced by other words. When a student wants to move a checker he or she must read the word on that checker before making a move or jumping a checker. This method is especially useful for beginning readers who need a great deal of repetition for skill mastery. For older students, to expand vocabulary, a player must give a different synonym if he or she moves the same checker for several consecutive plays. Two sets of words can be made by using both sides of the checkers with different color printing or labels for each side. Adhesive circle labels are particularly suitable.

word in both directions for younger students

Formats/Directions/And Basic Game Guidelines

- Cover the checker board with clear adhesive paper. Now you can tape task cards or adhesive labels on the appropriate squares. These can be removed from the board when you wish to use it for reinforcing another skill or other vocabulary.

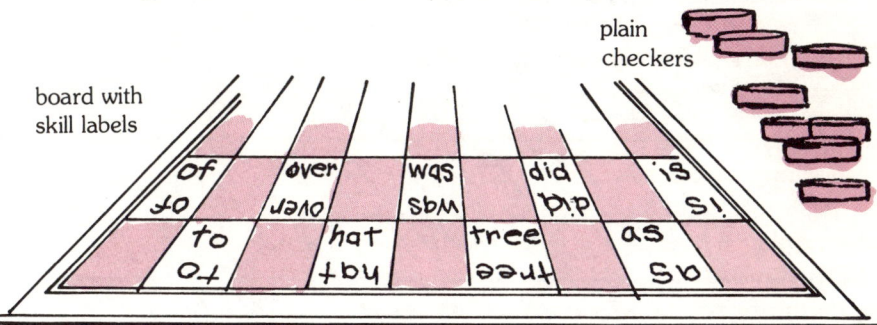

- Instead of taping task cards or labels on a board, simply construct skill task cards and stack them (face down) beside the board. Before a player can move a checker he or she must take the top card and successfully complete the task. If the player can not, then the opponent can have a free turn *if* he or she can successfully complete the task. Word-bank cards or skill flash cards could be used also.

- Students at different levels of word recognition or other skill development can play together simply by placing the word or skill tasks for each student facing the respective player.

Games As Learning Tools

2. To simplify checkers and to add an additional element of chance, include spaces with non-skill tasks such as *free move* or *extra turn*.

3. Don't hesitate to construct and use an over-size checkerboard when appropriate. In this way you can place larger task cards on the squares (containing sentences, quotations, etc.), and get more active involvement on the part of the players as they move the over-size checker pieces. Plastic-can covers, from dog food or coffee cans, make appropriate size checkers.

4. Answer keys can be useful for checkers games.

Formats/Directions/And Basic Game Guidelines

Summary Chart: CHECKERS

LEVEL	VOCABULARY	CONCEPTS AND FACTS	WORD ANALYSIS	GRAPHIC-SYMBOLIC
PRIMARY (Grades K-2)	Lang. Arts: Complete sentences using context clues <u>Give-The-Word Checkers</u> p. 99	Math.: Identify correct numerical values <u>What's The Number?</u> p. 110	Lang. Arts: Identify consonant blends, give example <u>Checker Blends</u> p. 121	Lang. Arts: Identify letters <u>Alphabet Checkers</u> p. 133
INTERMEDIATE (Grades 3-5)	Science: Define weather vocabulary <u>Weather Wordo</u> p. 102	Soc. Studies: Identify major invention of inventors <u>Inventor Checkers</u> p. 113	Lang. Arts: Add prefix or suffix to root words <u>Add-N-Affix</u> p. 124	Soc. Studies: Identify types of houses with country <u>House Hunt</u> p. 137
MIDDLE (Grades 6-8)	Foreign Lang.: Translate words to English <u>Word Wise</u> p. 105	Soc. Studies: Identify state capitals <u>What's The Place?</u> p. 116	Lang. Arts: Divide words into syllables <u>Syllable Checkers</u> p. 128	Soc. Studies: Identify map symbols <u>Map Hunt</u> p. 139
SENIOR (Grades 9-12)	Am. Gov't.: Identify synonyms for government terms <u>Politico</u> p. 107	English Lit.: Identify character and quote <u>Lit. Facts</u> p. 118	Foreign Lang.: Conjugate verbs <u>Verbe Checkers</u> p. 130	Drivers' Ed.: Identify, define road signs <u>Safe Driving</u> p. 141

Games As Learning Tools

CONCENTRATION

Concentration Game Directions:

This game consists of matching pairs of cards which have a common element depending upon the skill being reinforced. A plastic mat, game board, or other device is marked off into equal-sized spaces. The matching pairs of cards are randomly placed face down on all the spaces. The player selects a card, turns it face up, and identifies it. Another card is then chosen by the same player and also placed face up. The player identifies this card and determines whether it matches the first. If it does, the player keeps the two and takes another turn. If it does not, the player turns both cards over to their original places face down. The next player proceeds in the same manner. The player with the most pairs wins.

Concentration Game Guidelines:

1. Concentration can be simplified by adjusting the number of spaces. Younger children might begin with a concentration board containing 6 to 8 pairs. Remember that Concentration involves a memory challenge, and players may become frustrated if too much is required of them. You might start with six pairs and gradually add on as players show they can handle the task.

2. Concentration may be adapted for total class use in several ways. For example, use a classroom bulletin board, set up as a reusable Concentration board as illustrated below:

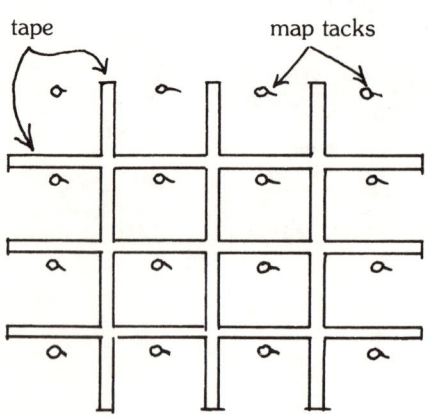

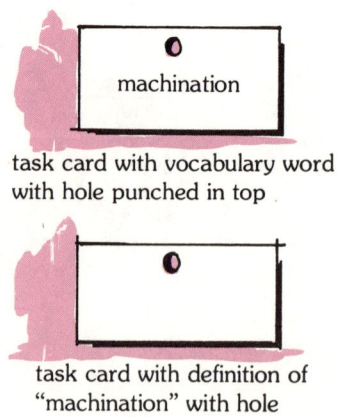

task card with vocabulary word with hole punched in top

task card with definition of "machination" with hole punched in top

Formats/Directions/And Basic Game Guidelines

You could also use an overhead transparency, resembling a Concentration board:

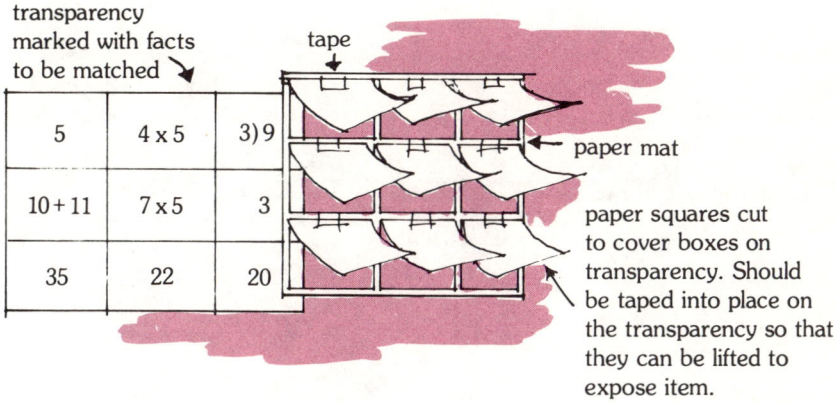

Some teachers also like to use the chalkboard as a Concentration board. Simply fold over standard size (8½ x 11) paper for each square and write the task item on the inside. Tape the paper items in squares on the chalkboard. This is especially easy to make, although it may not be reusable.

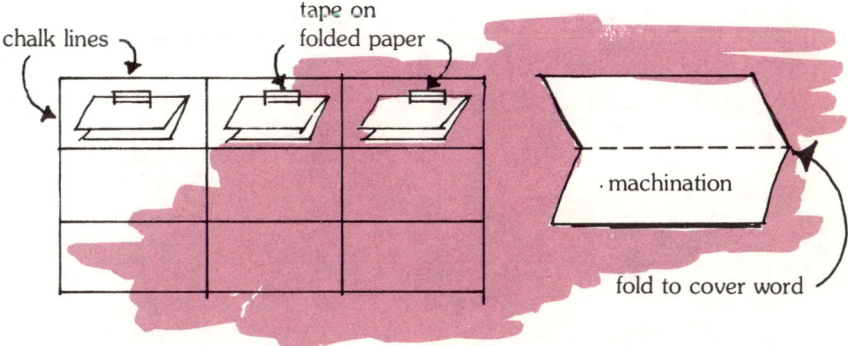

3. Some students, especially younger children, may not seem to pick up the strategy of remembering where the cards are by observing the cards other players turn over. Although this game-playing strategy is useful, many students use a random strategy to match pairs and have fun doing just that. Remember that your major focus is on reinforcing concepts and skills rather than on developing game-playing strategies.

Games As Learning Tools

Summary Chart: CONCENTRATION

LEVEL	VOCABULARY	CONCEPTS AND FACTS	WORD ANALYSIS	GRAPHIC-SYMBOLIC
PRIMARY (Grades K-2)	Math.: Match similar math terms <u>Math Pairs</u> p. 100	Soc. Studies: Match holiday symbols <u>Holiday Concentration</u> p. 111	Lang. Arts: Match words beginning with same blends <u>Blend Search</u> p. 122	Science: Match weather pictures <u>Weather Watch</u> p. 134
INTERMEDIATE (Grades 3-5)	Lang. Arts: match antonyms <u>Opposites Concentration</u> p. 103	Science: Match and label category of animal types <u>Animal Categories</u> p. 114	Lang. Arts: Identify words with same endings <u>Ending Concentration</u> p. 125	Math.: match geometric symbols with terms <u>Geo Term</u> p. 137
MIDDLE (Grades 6-8)	Math.: Match measurement terms of same quantity <u>Measure Match</u> p. 106	Science: Match shape and name of trees <u>Leaf Look</u> p. 117	Lang. Arts: Match root word with root + prefix, meanings <u>Roots And Prefixes</u> p. 128	Math.: Match dimensions with geometric shapes <u>Dimensions</u> p. 139
SENIOR (Grades 9-12)	Geometry: Match terms with definitions <u>Geo</u> p. 108	Soc. Studies: Match world leader with country <u>Leaders</u> p. 119	Lang. Arts: Dictionary Usage/spelling with diacritical markings <u>Dicto-Mark</u> p. 130	Home Econ.: Match pattern symbols with sewing directions <u>Stitch And Sew</u> p. 141

Formats/Directions/And Basic Game Guidelines

DOMINOES

Dominoes Game Directions:

The object of the game is for each player to get rid of all his or her dominoes by matching these dominoes with those face up on the board. The version of dominoes suited for most students is the one that calls for limiting the number of dominoes for play. All dominoes are placed face down in the center of the table. Players then draw dominoes according to the number playing. For two players each draws seven dominoes; for three or four players, each draws five. The remaining dominoes are called the 'boneyard'. One 'bone' from the 'boneyard' is turned face up.

For the first play a player matches the face-up domino in one of several ways:

    exact match, shape to shape.

A blank can be matched to any face regardless of how it has been previously played.

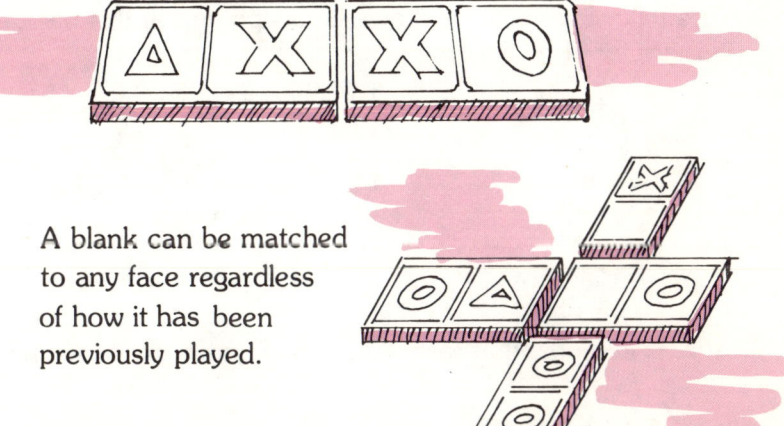

Each player in succession matches one domino to the face-up dominoes. If he or she cannot make a match, that player draws from the boneyard until he or she can. When there are no more dominoes in the boneyard, a player who cannot make a match passes. The winner is the first person to use all his or her dominoes or, if no further matches can be made, the player with the fewest dominoes.

Dominoes Game Guidelines:

1. Either commercial or teacher-made domino sets can be utilized.

    When commercial sets are used, skill tasks may be placed on adhesive labels and placed on the faces of the dominoes.

Games As Learning Tools

Teacher-made sets can be made on file cards or cardboard ranging in size from regular to oversize depending on the age of the players. Teacher-made domino sets should be protected with clear adhesive paper or plastic spray.

2. Skill tasks for sets should follow the basic domino frequency pattern:

0-0	0-0	1-0	2-0	3-0	4-0	5-0	6-0
1-1	1-0	1-1	2-1	3-1	4-1	5-1	6-1
2-2	2-0	2-1	2-2	3-2	4-2	5-2	6-2
3-3	3-0	3-1	2-3	3-3	4-3	5-3	6-3
4-4	4-0	4-1	2-4	3-4	4-4	5-4	6-4
5-5	5-0	5-1	2-5	3-5	4-5	5-5	6-5
6-6	6-0	6-1	2-6	3-6	4-6	5-6	6-6

The following example shows an adaptation of this basic domino pattern for skill reinforcement:

0- (blank)		1-0	run — (blank)
1 - run		1-1	run — run
2 - sit		1-2	run — sit
3 - hot		1-3	run — hot
4 - bed		1-4	run — bed
5 - had		1-5	run — had
6 - get		1-6	run — get

It is essential that tasks have ample number of matches.

3. If commercial dominoes are used, each player stands his or her dominoes on edge so only that player can view his or her dominoes. If cardboard or tagboard dominoes are utilized, a simple paper stand can be made by folding a 6" x 12" piece of oaktag in the following manner:

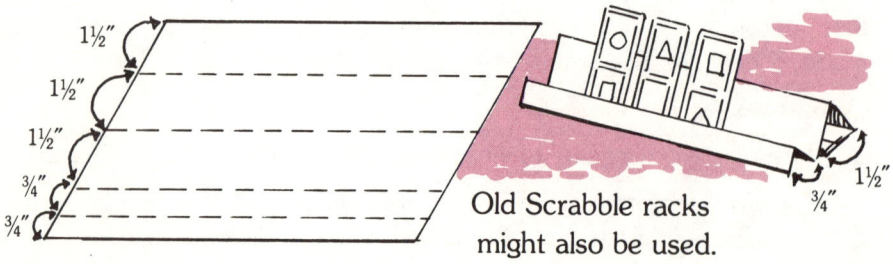

Old Scrabble racks might also be used.

Formats/Directions/And Basic Game Guidelines

4. Whenever pictures are used on dominoes the pictures should be reviewed with the students before the game is played.

5. A domino game may be made more complex by the substitution of tasks of increasing difficulty. For example, a game matching pictures may have a second set of dominoes which match words with the pictures:

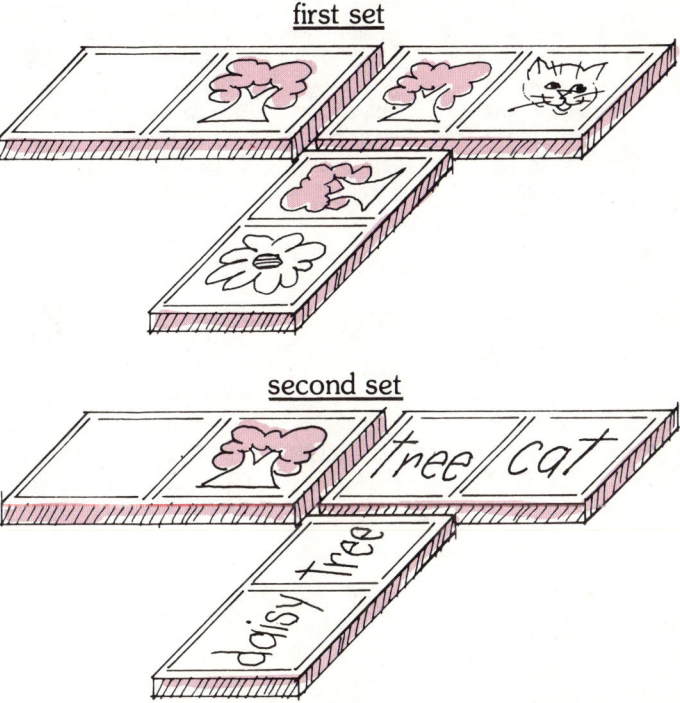

6. Since domino games are easy to make, students might make sets for each other or take them home for after-school reinforcement activities.

Games As Learning Tools

Summary Chart: DOMINOES

LEVEL	VOCABULARY	CONCEPTS AND FACTS	WORD ANALYSIS	GRAPHIC-SYMBOLIC
PRIMARY (Grades K-2)	Lang. Arts: Match closed vowel and appropriate final "e" words <u>Magic "e" Dominoes</u> p. 100	Lang. Arts: Match picture of whole object with part of whole object <u>Object Dominoes</u> p. 111	Lang. Arts: Match pictures of objects with same final consonant sound <u>End Sound</u> p. 122	Math.: Match clock face with written time <u>Tell-Time</u> p. 134
INTERMEDIATE (Grades 3-5)	Lang. Arts: Match cursive words with manuscript words <u>Word-Alike Dominoes</u> p. 103	Math.: Match multiplication facts <u>Multiplication Dominoes</u> p. 114	Any Content Area: Match words that go in same category <u>Word Attack Dominoes</u> p. 125	Soc. Studies: Match map symbols with meanings <u>Map Signs</u> p. 137
MIDDLE (Grades 6-8)	Any Content Area: Match word with definition <u>Definition Dominoes</u> p. 106	Soc. Studies: Match historical event with date <u>Date-Match</u> p. 117	Lang. Arts: Match words according to syllabication pattern <u>Divide-A-Word</u> p. 128	Foreign Lang.: Match symbols with foreign term <u>Le Symbol</u> p. 140
SENIOR (Grades 9-12)	Home Econ.: Match description of ingredients with product <u>Food-O Dominoes</u> p. 108	Science: (Biology) Match anatomical terms with their biological functions <u>Anatomy Dominoes</u> p. 119	Any Content Area: Match words of equal syllable units <u>Equal Syllables</u> p. 130	Chemistry: Match formulas with names <u>Chem Facts</u> p. 142

Formats/Directions/And Basic Game Guidelines

BOARD GAMES

Board Game Directions:

Games designed to be played on a board have spaces marked off in a sequential pattern upon which the players move from one fixed point to another. A die or spinner is usually the means to determine the number of spaces a player may advance after successfully performing a skill task. Each player moves his or her marker around the board in turn until one player is designated the winner by reaching the finishing point. Chance elements must be built into board games.

Board Game Guidelines:

1. There are several ways to include chance elements:
   - A task card may include the assigned move.

   > Do you have a final e word?
   > Move five spaces and
   > take an extra turn.

   - Separate non-skill chance cards may be drawn if the player lands on designated chance spaces either on the board or on the spinner, or if the player gets a double on dice that have been thrown.

   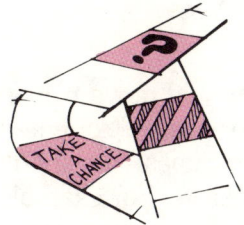

   Such chance cards may have a special place on the board. Chance spaces can be indicated by "Take a chance," or a picture, or spaces of a specified color.

   - The non-skill chance card directions may contain such items as: "Move ahead two spaces," or "Miss one turn," or "Take another turn after going two spaces," or "Move to the purple space ahead."

Games As Learning Tools

- These non-skill chance card tasks might also follow the theme motif of the game. For example, in an auto race game the task might be "Take a pit stop and miss one turn." Or, in a safari-theme game the task might be "Move ahead four spaces to escape the charging bull elephant."

skill task cards
chance cards
designated chance spaces

- Chance spaces can be included on a spinner.

2. Generally non-skill chance spaces or cards should move players ahead or provide extra turns, rather than being negatively oriented. While negative chances have a place in learning games, they should be limited with the higher proportion being positive. For example,

positively oriented:

Take an extra turn
Move ahead one space
Move to the next red space

negatively oriented:

Lose a turn
Move back one space

Formats/Directions/And Basic Game Guidelines

3. A game board can also have alternate paths, a shorter path having fewer spaces but more deterrents while the longer one includes more opportunities to advance faster.

4. To increase the versatility of game boards, do not permanently affix skill tasks (such as vocabulary words) to the board. Instead, try:
   - *peel-off adhesive labels,* to place on spaces. These can be easily removed and replaced for additional skill reinforcement.
   - *task cards,* to be placed on or beside the board. These cards can contain appropriate words, questions, or skill tasks.

5. Tie your board games into specific curricular content and add interest by affixing theme pictures, drawings, and slogans to the game board. (See pages 42 and 46)

6. Whenever pictures are used for skill task cards be sure to go over with the students what the pictures represent.

7. Answer keys should be provided whenever possible so that the game does not have to be supervised. In such cases, the task cards are numbered to match the answer key.

8. Since the number of players may vary, you will need to pace the game by deciding the maximum number of spaces a player may advance at one time. Effective pacing of a game may take several trial plays. For example:

- with four to six players
    use dice or a 6-10 spinner
    (since they need to advance
    faster with fewer plays),

- with two or three players
    use one die or a 1-5 spinner
    (since they have more chances
    to take a turn).

9. Vary the number of spaces on a game board according to the needs and ages of your students. Usually fewer spaces are suitable for younger children or poor achievers.

Games As Learning Tools

10. Clear adhesive paper is usually the best protection for game board surfaces. Clear adhesive paper or clear adhesive spray may be used on skill task and chance cards, depending on the nature of their construction. Covering backs of game boards with matching decorative adhesive paper used on game parts boxes aids in storing games. (See page 53 for final steps in constructing games.)

11. Some games may not be completed in the allotted time. It may be necessary to declare the winner as the player closest to the finish.

12. Groups of students can be involved in board game activities through the use of overhead transparencies. In the following example, two teams of students in a French class participate in throwing dice and progressing along the road on the transparency by moving markers or by using felt-tip pens to indicate position. Either shows clearly on the projected image for total class involvement.

BON VOYAGE: A Trip Through France

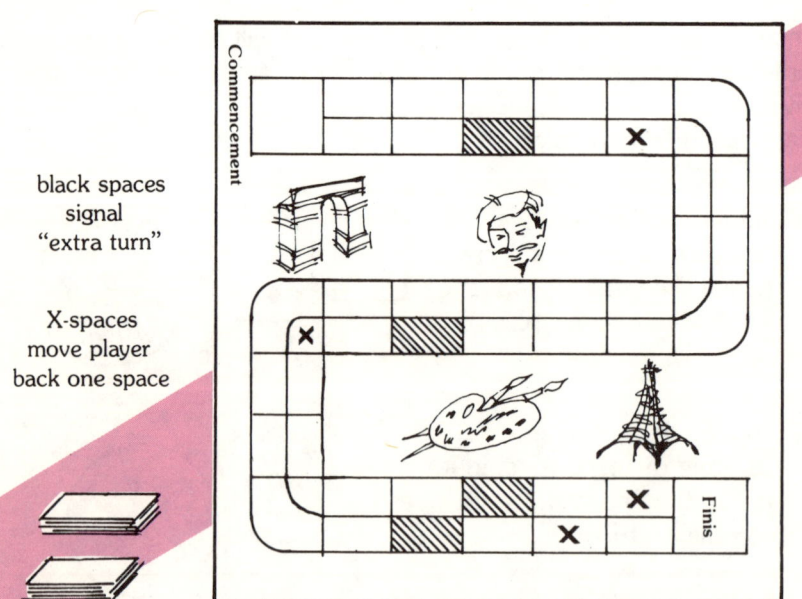

black spaces signal "extra turn"

X-spaces move player back one space

Task cards consist of French-to-English translation skills.

(Adapted from an idea by Mary Schwartz, Prince Georges County)

Formats/Directions/And Basic Game Guidelines

Summary Chart: BOARD GAMES

LEVEL	VOCABULARY	CONCEPTS AND FACTS	WORD ANALYSIS	GRAPHIC-SYMBOLIC
PRIMARY (Grades K-2)	Lang. Arts: Make compound words from single words p. 100	Math.: Identify numerical value with coin names p. 111	Lang. Arts: Give word with same medial vowel p. 122	Lang. Arts: Identify traffic signs, give meaning p. 134
INTERMEDIATE (Grades 3-5)	Phys. Educ.: Identify correct term for sports activity p. 103	Lang. Arts: Correctly answer questions about medicine labels p. 114	Lang. Arts: Provide appropriate affix when root word is given in context p. 125	Lang. Arts: (Punctuation) Read sentences with proper intonation p. 137
MIDDLE (Grades 6-8)	Soc. Studies: Identify term for geographical land or water masses p. 106	Lang. Arts: Read sentence and identify its structure type p. 117	Foreign Lang.: Provide correct form of highlighted key word in sentence p. 129	Home Econ.: Identify measurement abbreviations p. 140
SENIOR (Grades 9-12)	English Lit.: Translate Old English terms into modern English p. 108	Math.: Solve algebraic equations p. 119	Lang. Arts: (Dictionary) Sequence words as to dictionary location p. 131	Phys. Educ.: Identify football referee's signals from picture cards p. 142

Games As Learning Tools

ACTIVE GAME FORMATS

Active Game Directions:

Basic formats for active games include circle, relay, and tag. However, games of the active type are usually unique in their directions for play, based on the concept or skills being developed, and cannot be generalized. Therefore, specific directions for each active game are given in Chapter 6 where the games are described in detail in terms of the concept or skills being developed, directions, scoring, and variations in skills application. Although these games are designed basically for the elementary grades, there may be occasions when they might be appropriately used with older students.

Formats/Directions/And Basic Game Guidelines

Active Game Guidelines:

1. Depending on the learning skills involved or the mechanics of the game, most active games are suited for playing by either large or small groups.

   - Whole-class participation can be used on the playground or in a multipurpose room.
   - Groups of eight to ten students can play within the classroom.
   - Often two circles or four teams can be utilized. However, for games involving greater levels of concentration and a corresponding need for supervision, you may want to limit both the size and the number of teams.

2. When assigning students to teams be sure they are of mixed ability levels so that play will be matched more evenly. In some cases you might want to make a rule that team help is permissable when a member of a team does not know an answer. It is important that students are not eliminated from the game; only scores might be affected.

3. If you are working with groups of varying achievement, you may include each group as a team. If you are reinforcing the same skill with each, you may provide different levels of related tasks for each group.
(See Letter Pattern Change on page 126)

4. In utilizing active games it is of prime importance to consider the developmental level of students both in terms of motor skills and following directions.

   - Students should be called upon to perform physically only those motor skills they can handle comfortably.
   - Directions for play should be simple enough for all students in the game to be able to follow, at least with guidance from team members.

Games As Learning Tools

5. At the conclusion of the game, students should be given an opportunity to evaluate the skills or concepts being learned in the game and how they played the game. Often in the excitement of an active game students forget they are reviewing some aspect of classwork. Evaluating will remind students that although they had fun they were also learning. Questions for evaluation might include:

> Did you like *Match The Sound?* (See page 123)
> How could we improve our playing of *Match The Sound?*
> Do you think you need more work with consonant blends?

6. The teacher or leader should adapt the game to the skills of the students. For example, when tossing a ball to a student who may not be able to catch very well, you should throw the ball as to assure the student's catching it. You might also count a bit slower, or wait a moment after calling out a word or holding up a word card, before tossing or bouncing a ball to give a less able student time to respond.

Formats/Directions/And Basic Game Guidelines

Summary Chart: ACTIVE GAMES

LEVEL	VOCABULARY	CONCEPTS AND FACTS	WORD ANALYSIS	GRAPHIC-SYMBOLIC
PRIMARY (Grades K-2)	Soc. Studies: Sight vocabulary recognition **Words In A Circle** (circle game) p. 100	Science: Movements of animals (hopping, jumping, etc.) **Going Home** (circle game) p. 112	Lang. Arts: Consonant blends, digraphs **Match The Sound** (circle game) p. 123	Lang. Arts: Visual color recognition **Rainbow** (circle game) p. 135
	Lang. Arts: Action words demonstrated **Action Relay** (relay game) p. 101	Science: Comprehension of weather terms **Weather Report** (relay game) p. 112	Lang. Arts: Initial consonant blend match **See The Same** (relay game) p. 123	Math: Visual discrimination of simple shapes **Shape Relay** (relay game) p. 135
	Lang. Arts: visual discrimination of whole words **Cross The Bridge** (tag game) p. 101	Math: Numbers and quantities **Number Tag** (tag game) p. 113	Lang. Arts: Recognition of initial consonant blends **Blend Tag** (tag game) p. 123	Lang. Arts: Visual discrimination of upper and lowercase letters **Alphabet Tag** (tag game) p. 136
INTERMEDIATE (Grades 3-5)	Lang. Arts: Rhyming words **Rhyme Chase** (circle game) p. 104	Math: Addition, subtraction, multiplication facts **Call Fact** (circle game) p. 115	Lang. Arts Number of syllables in words **Syllables In A Basket** (circle game) p. 126	Science: Visual discrimination of cloud formations **What-It-It Relay** (relay game) p. 138
	Soc. Studies: Map terms and definitions **Word Erase** (relay game) p. 104	Math: Coin values **Banker And The Coins** (relay game) p. 115	Lang. Arts: Open and closed syllable patterns **Letter Pattern** (relay game) p. 126	
	Lang. Arts: Sight vocabulary **Find-A-Word** (stunt game) p. 104			

Games As Learning Tools

Which games should I use?

Having an understanding of and ideas for using basic game formats now enables you to begin your implementation of learning games as a teaching strategy. Making decisions as to what games to use requires a careful look at (1) your students, (2) your objectives, and (3) your classroom organizational constraints. These considerations have been discussed earlier in Chapters 2 and 3, but the following key questions are useful as you make appropriate decisions:

Consider your students:

- What are their interests?
- Do I want them to work in pairs, small groups, or as an entire class?
- Can they work cooperatively with little supervision?
- Can they follow game directions?

Consider your objectives:

- Does my objective lend itself to a learning game?
- Is one game format more effective than another for this objective?

Consider your classroom organization:

- Do I have space to play the game?
- Do I have time to play the game?
- How can I organize my instructional plans to accommodate games?

Chapter 6

Game Ideas

How do I get ideas for games in my specific subject area? What kinds of content skills can be developed and reinforced at my grade level?

This chapter describes specific game ideas for classroom use. The chapter is organized according to the four content skills that cut across all subject areas as presented in Chapter 6:

<u>Vocabulary</u> — activities which develop and reinforce meaningful vocabulary in the subject areas.

<u>Concepts and Facts</u> — activities which reinforce concepts and facts in subject areas.

<u>Word Analysis</u> — activities which reinforce word attack skills, word parts, or spelling patterns for dealing with unfamiliar words in subject-area reading materials.

<u>Graphic-Symbolic Skills</u> — activities which reinforce non-verbal symbols and their meanings in the various subject areas.

It was felt that these four content skills are essential in all subject areas and lend themselves well to learning games in both the passive and active formats. Within each skill area, games and their variations are grouped according to the following four levels of difficulty:

<u>Primary Level</u> — appropriate for students in grades K-2

<u>Intermediate Level</u> — appropriate for students in grades 3-5

<u>Middle Level</u> — appropriate for students in grades 6-8

<u>Senior Level</u> — appropriate for students in grades 9-12

Games As Learning Tools

Of course, there is much overlap between these levels, and knowing your students remains the best guide for your final selection. For example, as a sixth grade teacher you may find some game ideas at the primary level which are appropriate for some of your students with special needs. By adapting them to more mature formats the same skills can be effectively developed and reinforced.

Variations are included for each game described. The suggested variations provide for two ways of adapting games. One way is adapting a game to different dimensions within the content skill itself. For example, a vocabulary game matching antonyms can be adapted to matching synonyms or matching a word with its definition. A second type of variation adapts a game to another subject area. For example, a vocabulary game suggested for developing science unit words can be adapted and used with math or social studies terms.

Variations or adaptations of games should be named to reflect the skill you are developing so that it will be easy to identify the game. For example, what is described as *Weather Wordo* (see page 102) as a checkers game to reinforce weather terms can be adapted to develop vocabulary relating to simple machines (lever, pulley, screw, etc.) and be named *Machino*.

How to Use this Chapter:

Game descriptions in this chapter differ according to whether they are passive or active. The *passive* games (bingo, card games, checkers, concentration, dominoes, board games) are outlined to describe the content skill to be developed or reinforced. Variations are also suggested for incorporating other content skills with other subject areas. Detailed descriptions as to how the basic games are played have been presented in Chapter 5 in order to eliminate repetition. However, descriptions of *active* games, in addition to identifying the content skills and possible variations, provide detailed directions for play unique to each game. Basic overall guidelines for using both passive and active games appear in Chapter 5. This is one way to begin:

- The charts for each skill area may serve as good starting points.
- Decide what skill you wish to reinforce.
- Identify the appropriate difficulty level.

Game Ideas

- Select a game and refer to its description in this chapter.
- Refer to Chapter 5 for specific helps in implementation of the game format selected.
- View these ideas as *starting points*. Feel free to adapt them or to create your own!

Games As Learning Tools

VOCABULARY

Game Title	Game Format (A — active)	Subject Area*	Game Descr.	Guide- lines
PRIMARY LEVEL (GRADES K-2)				
Opposites Bingo	Bingo	Lang. Arts	p. 99	p. 61
Color Match	Card Game	Lang. Arts	p. 99	p. 65
Give-The-Word Checkers	Checkers	Lang. Arts	p. 99	p. 74
Math Pairs	Concentration	Math.	p. 100	p. 78
Magic 'e' Dominoes	Dominoes	Lang. Arts	p. 100	p. 81
(compound words)	Board Game	Lang. Arts	p. 100	p. 85
Words In A Circle	Circle Game — A	Soc. Studies	p. 100	p. 91
Action Relay	Relay Game — A	Lang. Arts	p. 101	p. 91
Cross The Bridge	Tag Game — A	Lang. Arts	p. 101	p. 91
INTERMEDIATE LEVEL (GRADES 3-5)				
Time-Line Bingo	Bingo	Soc. Studies	p. 102	p. 61
Phrase Match	Card Game	Lang. Arts	p. 102	p. 69
Weather Wordo	Checkers	Science	p. 102	p. 74
Opposites Concentration	Concentration	Lang. Arts	p. 103	p. 78
Word-Alike Dominoes	Dominoes	Lang. Arts	p. 103	p. 81
(sports terms)	Board Game	Phys. Educ.	p. 103	p. 85
Rhyme Chase	Circle Game — A	Lang. Arts	p. 104	p. 91
Word Erase	Relay Game — A	Soc. Studies	p. 104	p. 91
Find-A-Word	Stunt Game — A	Lang. Arts	p. 104	p. 91
MIDDLE LEVEL (GRADES 6-8)				
Clue Bingo	Bingo	Lang. Arts	p. 105	p. 61
Category Rummy	Card Game	Science	p. 105	p. 64
Word Wise	Checkers	Foreign Lang.	p. 105	p. 74
Measure Match	Concentration	Math.	p. 106	p. 78
Definition Dominoes	Dominoes	Any Subject	p. 106	p. 81
(geographical terms)	Board Game	Soc. Studies	p. 106	p. 85
SENIOR LEVEL (GRADES 9-12)				
Auto Bingo	Bingo	Ind. Arts	p. 107	p. 61
History Poker	Card Game	Am. Hist.	p. 107	p. 66
Politico	Checkers	Am. Govt.	p. 107	p. 74
Geo	Concentration	Geometry	p. 108	p. 78
Food-O Dominoes	Dominoes	Home Econ.	p. 108	p. 81
(Old English terms)	Board Game	Eng. Lit.	p. 108	p. 85

*Although examples are described in terms of specific subject area, variations are also included.

Game Ideas

VOCABULARY
Primary Level (Grades K-2)

OPPOSITES BINGO
Format: Bingo (page 61)
Subject Area: Language Arts
Players: 2 to whole class

Directions: Caller reads words. Players match with opposite words on their bingo cards. For example:

Caller reads:	Player matches on card:
high	low
smooth	rough

Variations: Animal names matched with animal categories on cards; match colors, shapes with names.

COLOR MATCH
Format: Card Game (page 65)
Subject Area: Language Arts
Players: two

Directions: Players match color cards with color-word cards.

Variations: Match numerals with number words; pictures with animal names; uppercase with lowercase letters.

GIVE-THE-WORD CHECKERS
Format: Checkers (page 74)
Subject Area: Language Arts
Players: two

Directions: With each turn a player inserts an appropriate word in sentences on task cards. For example:

Task Card:	Player may say:
I live in a _____ .	I live in a <u>house</u>.

Variations: Use science and math sentences.

Games As Learning Tools

MATH PAIRS Format: Concentration (page 78)
Subject Area: Math Players: 2 to whole class

<u>Directions</u>: Players read and match math terms. For example:

<u>Appropriate match might include:</u>
plus — add   greater than — >

<u>Variations</u>: Match colors; shapes; numerals; number words.

MAGIC 'E' DOMINOES Format: Dominoes (page 81)
Subject Area: Language Arts Players: 2 to 4

<u>Directions</u>: Players match final 'e' words with corresponding closed-vowel words. Player must read words so matched. For example:

<u>Appropriate matches might include:</u>

	ride	mad
pine	rid	
pin		

<u>Variations</u>: Match different number syllable words; colors; shapes; numbers.

(Use any game board) Format: Board Game (page 85)
Subject Area: Language Arts Players: 2 to 4

<u>Directions</u>: Players make a compound word from a single word on the task card before advancing. The word on the task card can be either the first or second half of the compound word. For example:

<u>Task Card:</u>   <u>Player may say:</u>
base   baseball

<u>Variations</u>: Use rhyming words; contractions; words and their definitions.

WORDS IN A CIRCLE[1] Format: Circle Game
Subject Area: Social Studies

<u>Directions</u>: Players form a circle facing the center. Using social studies unit terms each student is given a word card. The cards are read and then placed on the floor in front of the players. At a signal the

---

[1] Adapted from Humphrey, James H., and Sullivan, Dorothy D.: <u>Teaching Slow Learners Through Active Games</u>. Springfield, Illinois: Charles C Thomas, 1970, pp. 77-78.

players march (hop, skip, jump, etc.) around the circle until signaled to stop. Each player should be standing by a card. Each time a player reads the word he or she is standing by and uses it in a sentence that player earns a point. If a player cannot read a word, the players on either side may help. Play continues until most words have been read by each player. The player with the highest score wins.

Variations: Numerals, shapes, and colors matched with words.

ACTION RELAY[2]   Format: Relay Game
Subject Area: Language Arts

Directions: Students are divided into several teams. The teams form rows ten to fifteen feet from a chalkboard. Duplicate lists of action words are written on the board, one for each team. The leader of each team runs to the board at a given signal, reads the first word, erases it, and performs the action of the word. The leader runs back to the team and touches the next player who then runs to the board to act out the second word in the same manner. A student who is having difficulty with a word should receive help from other members of the team. Play continues until the first team completing all words correctly wins.

CROSS THE BRIDGE[3]   Format: Tag Game
Subject Area: Language Arts

Directions: Two lines are marked off at opposite ends of a playing area. One student is designated as the Bridge Keeper and stands in the center. Each player is given a word card and all players stand at one end of the playing area. The Bridge Keeper has a box containing duplicates of the players' words. The players call "Bridge Keeper, may we use the bridge? May we use the bridge?" The Bridge Keeper answers, "Yes, if your have [see] ." All players who have [see] try to get across the line at the other end of the playing area before being tagged by the Bridge Keeper. Players who are caught stay with the Bridge Keeper to help catch other players. Those not caught return to the original side to continue play until only one person is left. The last player then becomes the Bridge Keeper.

Variations: The Bridge Keeper may hold a card up and may read the word to extend word recognition; colors or shapes might also be used.

---

[2]Ibid. pp. 86-87. (Adapted)
[3]Ibid. p. 67 (Adapted)

VOCABULARY
Intermediate Level (Grades 3-5)

TIME-LINE BINGO Format: Bingo (page 61)
Subject Area: Social Studies Players: 2 to whole class

Directions: The Caller reads descriptions of "time-line" terms. Players match with correct terms on their cards. For example:

Caller reads:	Player matches on card:
ten years	decade
1000 years	millennium

Variations: Subject-area word definitions matched with word; pictures of animals matched with categories (mammals, bird, fish, etc.); pictures of different modes of transportation matched with transportation terms.

PHRASE MATCH Format: Card Game (page 65)
Subject Area: Language Arts Players: 3 or 4

Directions: Players match beginning and ending phrases to complete a sentence. For example:

Appropriate matches might include:
 I am going — to the barber shop
 After school — I play with my friends

Variations: Match science statements with cause and effect relationships ("Cumulus clouds" — "indicate fair weather"); match social studies statements ("Columbus discovered America" — "looking for the Far East").

WEATHER WORDO Format: Checkers (page 74)
Subject Area: Science Players: two

Directions: With each turn a player reads the weather word on a task card and then defines the words. For example:

Task Card:	Player may say:
precipitation	-approprite meaning or
nimbus	identification of each
tornado	term

Variations: Vocabulary and definitions from any subject area can be used.

Game Ideas

OPPOSITES CONCENTRATION
Format: Concentration (page 78)
Subject Area: Language Arts
Players: 2 to whole class

Directions: Players match two words that are antonyms. For example:

Appropriate matches might include:
- condense - expand
- passive - active
- obscure - famous
- difficult - easy

Variations: Use antonyms and synonyms in the respective subject areas.

WORD-ALIKE DOMINOES
Format: Dominoes (page 81)
Subject Area: Language Arts
Players: 2 to 4

Directions: Players match cursive words to manuscript words. Words must be read before the player can use the domino. For example:

Appropriate matches might include:
- seventeen — *seventeen*
- happiness — *happiness*

Variations: Match foreign and English words; antonyms and synonyms.

(Use any game board)
Format: Board Game (page 85)
Subject Area: Physical Education
Players: 2 to 4

Directions: Players must identify correct term for a description of a certain type of action in a sport. If correct, the players may advance around the board. For example:

Task Card:
Basketball:
to bounce the ball while moving on the court

Player may say:
dribble

Variations: Use descriptions of geographical land and water formations with words; weather conditions with words; math processes with words.

Games As Learning Tools

RHYME CHASE[4] Format: Circle Game
Subject Area: Language Arts

<u>Directions</u>: The students are given a word card with a familiar vocabulary word written on it as they form a circle. Each player reads the word on the card. The Caller then reads a word. All the players who have a word that rhymes with the word called must run to a previously designated safe space. All other players in the circle try to tag the runners. A point is given to any player tagged. The player with the lowest number of points is the winner.

WORD ERASE[5] Format: Relay Game
Subject Area: Social Studies

<u>Directions</u>: Players are divided into two teams and form rows ten to fifteen feet from a chalkboard. Identical lists of science vocabulary terms are written on the board. The Caller reads a definition and then gives a signal. The first player on each team runs to the board, calls out the defined word and erases it. A point is scored for the team that erases the correct word first. Play continues in the same manner with the second player on each team erasing the next defined word. The team with the most points wins.

FIND-A-WORD Format: Stunt Game
Subject Area: Language Arts

<u>Directions</u>: Words are placed in a box. The Leader calls "Nancy, can you hop to the box and find the word *carpenter*?" The student hops to the box, finds *carpenter* and uses it in a sentence. "John, can you skip to the box and find the word *pliable*?" For each word found and used correctly in a sentence, the player scores one point. Movements may include waddle, run, jump, skate, etc. It is suggested that a small group be assigned to this game so that players won't have to wait long for their turn. A time limit may be set with an egg timer or by counting to five. This game could be adapted for team play by having duplicate boxes of words.

---

[4]Ibid. p. 64. (Adapted)
[5]Ibid. p. 77. (Adapted)

VOCABULARY
Middle Level (Grades 6-8)

CLUE BINGO
Subject Area: Language Arts

Format: Bingo (page 61)
Players: 2 to whole class

Directions: Caller reads meaning "clue" (such as from crossword puzzles). Players match with correct terms on their cards. For example:

Caller reads:	Player matches on card:
masculine being	male

Variations: Social studies or science "clues" are matched with unit vocabulary.

CATEGORY RUMMY
Subject Area: Science

Format: Card Game (page 64)
Players: 2 to 4

Directions: Players categorize and label vocabulary cards. For example:

Appropriate categories might include:
nimbus + cirrus + stratus + cumulus = cloud forms
tornado + cyclone + hurricane = storms

Variations: Math measurement terms (liquid, linear, etc.); words with different numbers of syllables; words grouped according to parts of speech. (Some words could be used in more than one category.)

WORD WISE
Subject Area: Foreign Language

Format: Checkers (page 74)
Players: two

Directions: Players read and translate words placed on checker board into English equivalents. For example:

Word on board:	Player may say:
vous	you
bonjour	good day
trois	three

Variations: Give an addition, subtraction, or multiplication statement for number appearing on board.

Games As Learning Tools

MEASURE MATCH
Subject Area: Math
Format: Concentration (page 78)
Players: 2 to whole class

<u>Directions</u>: Players match terms that equal the same measurement quantity. For example:

<u>Appropriate matches might include</u>:
- 4 pints - 2 quarts
- 10 centimeters - 1 decimeter
- 2000 lbs. - 1 ton
- 8 quarts - 1 peck

<u>Variations</u>: Match products with countries; characters with books.

DEFINITION DOMINOES
Subject Area: Any Subject
Format: Dominoes (page 81)
Players: 2 to 4

<u>Directions</u>: Players match terms with definitions. For example:

<u>Appropriate matches might include</u>:
meteor — solid particle from heavenly body

<u>Variations</u>: Match authors with book titles; artists with famous paintings.

(Use any board game)
Subject Area: Geography
Format: Board Game (page 85)
Players: 2 to 4

<u>Directions</u>: Players must identify term for land and water masses on task card before advancing around the board. For example:

<u>Task Card</u>:   <u>Player may say</u>:
body of land surrounded by water on all sides   island

<u>Variations</u>: Use descriptions of weather conditions with weather terms.

VOCABULARY
Senior Level (Grades 9-12)

AUTO BINGO Format: Bingo (page 61)
Subject Area: Industrial Arts Players: 2 to whole class

<u>Directions</u>: Caller points to numbered parts of an automobile engine on a large chart. Players match with correct labels for the engine parts on their cards. For example:

<u>Caller points to</u>:   <u>Player matches on card</u>:
   air filter (picture)   air filter (word)
   distributor cap   distributor cap

<u>Variations</u>: Match foreign with English terms.

HISTORY POKER Format: Card Game (page 66)
Subject Area: American History Players: 2 to 7

<u>Directions</u>: Players try to form groupings of their terms. For example:

<u>Appropriate grouping might include</u>:
underground railroad + bondage + servitude + emancipation = pertaining to slavery

<u>Variations</u>: Categorize other subject-area terms.

POLITICO Format: Checkers (page 74)
Subject Area: American Government Players: two

<u>Directions</u>: Players read and identify government terms placed on checker board. For example:

<u>Word on board</u>:   <u>Player may say</u>:
   caucus   —acceptable meanings
   gerrymandering   or synonyms

<u>Variations</u>: Define or describe terms from other subject areas.

Games As Learning Tools

GEO
Subject Area: Geometry
Format: Concentration (page 78)
Players: 2 to whole class

<u>Directions</u>: Players match vocabulary terms with correct definitions. For example:

<u>Appropriate matches might include</u>:
- spheroid — solid figure resembling a sphere but not perfectly round
- rectangle — a parallelogram, all of whose angles are right angles

<u>Variations</u>: Match any other subject-area terms and definitions.

FOOD-O DOMINOES
Subject Area: Home Economics
Format: Dominoes (page 81)
Players: 2 to 4

<u>Directions</u>: Players match products with ingredients. For example:

<u>Appropriate matches might include</u>:
Ingredients: peppers, onions, cumin seed, garlic, oregano, caraway
Product: chili powder

<u>Variations</u>: In shop classes match pictures and names of various tools.

(Use any board game)
Subject Area: English Literature
Format: Board Game (page 85)
Players: 2 to 6

<u>Directions</u>: Players must translate Old English term on task card into modern English. If correct, the players advance. For example:

<u>Task Card</u>:	<u>Player may say</u>:
prithee	pray thee, please
thralldom	servitude

<u>Variations</u>: Translate slang terms or Black English into formal English.

Game Ideas

CONCEPTS AND FACTS

Game Title	Game Format (A — active)	Subject Area*	Game Descr.	Guide-lines
PRIMARY LEVEL (GRADES K-2)				
Animal Bingo	Bingo	Science	p. 110	p. 61
Math Rummy	Card Game	Math.	p. 110	p. 64
What's The Number?	Checkers	Math.	p. 110	p. 74
Holiday Concentration	Concentration	Soc. Studies	p. 111	p. 78
Object Dominoes	Dominoes	Lang. Arts	p. 111	p. 81
(coin values)	Board Game	Math.	p. 111	p. 85
Going Home	Circle Game — A	Science	p. 112	p. 91
Weather Report	Relay Game — A	Science	p. 112	p. 91
Number Tag	Tag Game — A	Math.	p. 113	p. 91
INTERMEDIATE LEVEL (GRADES 3-5)				
State-O	Bingo	Soc. Studies	p. 113	p. 61
Sentence Rummy	Card Game	Lang. Arts	p. 113	p. 64
Inventor Checkers	Checkers	Soc. Studies	p. 113	p. 74
Animal Categories	Concentration	Science	p. 114	p. 78
Multiplication Dominoes	Dominoes	Math.	p. 114	p. 81
(medicine labels)	Board Game	Lang. Arts	p. 114	p. 85
Call Fact	Circle Game — A	Math.	p. 115	p. 91
Banker And The Coins	Relay Game — A	Math.	p. 115	p. 91
MIDDLE LEVEL (GRADES 6-8)				
Guess Who	Bingo	Soc. Studies	p. 116	p. 61
Le Bag	Card Game	Foreign Lang.	p. 116	p. 70
What's The Place?	Checkers	Soc. Studies	p. 116	p. 74
Leaf Look	Concentration	Science	p. 117	p. 78
Date-Match	Dominoes	Soc. Studies	p. 117	p. 81
(sentence structure)	Board Game	Lang. Arts	p. 117	p. 85
SENIOR LEVEL (GRADES 9-12)				
Job Hunt	Bingo	Lang. Arts	p. 118	p. 61
Know Your Art	Card Game	Art	p. 118	p. 69
Lit Facts	Checkers	Eng. Lit.	p. 118	p. 74
Leaders	Concentration	Soc. Studies	p. 119	p. 78
Anatomy Dominoes	Dominoes	Science	p. 119	p. 81
(algebraic equations)	Board Game	Math.	p. 119	p. 85

*Although examples are described in terms of specific subject area, variations are also included.

Games As Learning Tools

CONCEPTS AND FACTS
Primary Level (Grades K-2)

ANIMAL BINGO   Format: Bingo (page 61)
Subject Area: Science   Players: 2 to whole class

<u>Directions</u>: Caller displays pictures of or names full-grown animals. Players match with correct name of baby animals on cards. For example:

Caller shows or reads:	Player matches on card:
horse	colt
deer	fawn

<u>Variations</u>: Pictures of common objects matched with shapes.

MATH RUMMY   Format: Card Game (page 64)
Subject Area: Math   Players: 2 to 4

<u>Directions</u>: Players form categories of four cards with the same number for the answer. For example:

<u>Appropriate category might include:</u>

     3 + 1   2 + 2   6 − 2   10 − 6

<u>Variations</u>: Match like-colors or numbers of objects on cards.

WHAT'S THE NUMBER?   Format: Checkers (page 74)
Subject Area: Math   Players: two

<u>Directions</u>: With each turn a player must identify the correct number of a set on the task card. For example:

Task Card:	Player may say:
X X X X X	5

Game Ideas

HOLIDAY CONCENTRATION   Format: Concentration (page 78)
Subject Area: Social Studies   Players: 2 to whole class

Directions: Players identify and match two holiday symbols. For example:

    Appropriate matches might include:
      Indian — Pilgrim   firecracker — American flag
      bunny — Easter basket   Menorah — seven-branch candelabra

Variations: Match clothing with various weather conditions; foods with appropriate serving containers.

OBJECT DOMINOES   Format: Dominoes (page 81)
Subject Area: Language Arts   Players: 2 to 4

Directions: Players match pictures of missing parts of familiar objects to pictures of objects with missing parts. For example:

    Appropriate matches might include:
      eyes — face without eyes
      shoe laces — shoes without shoe laces
      flower — flower stalk

Variations: Match parts of objects; match numbers or letters in sequence.

(Use any board game)   Format: Board Game (page 85)
Subject Area: Math   Players: 2 to 4

Directions: Players identify the name of a coin with its numerical value on the task card before advancing around the board. For example:

Task Card:	Player may say:
quarter	25¢
one dollar, one fifty-cent piece	$1.50

Variations: Name appropriate article of clothing to wear for picture of weather condition on task card; identify number of objects pictured on task card which could also determine the number of spaces to move.

Games As Learning Tools

GOING HOME
Subject Area: Science

Format: Circle Game

<u>Directions</u>: Players form a single circle facing center. Team A and Team B are selected by designating every other student A or B. The Caller says "The (geese or kangaroos) are going home." First Team A, and then Team B, exchange places within the circle by imitating the movement that the animal would make going home. For example, geese would flap their arms in a flying motion, kangaroos would jump. Teams score a point for each player who successfully changes places without being caught by the Caller.

WEATHER REPORT
Subject Area: Science

Format: Relay Game

<u>Directions</u>: Two teams face two large felt figures on a flannel board. An assortment of identical clothing is placed around each figure. The Caller gives a simple weather report. For example: "Today will be sunny and fair. High temperatures will be in the nineties." At a given signal, the first player on each team runs to the board and appropriately dresses the figure. One point is given for each piece of appropriate clothing. Note: This game encourages decision-making and also stresses listening comprehension.

NUMBER TAG
Subject Area: Math

Format: Tag Game

<u>Directions</u>: Players on two teams stand facing each other in two lines fifteen to twenty feet apart. Players wear cards with different numbers of objects on them. The Caller calls out a number or holds up a card with a number of objects on it. All players who have the same quantity of objects run to change places before the Caller can tag them. Teams score points for each player who is not caught. The Caller may change places with any player caught.

CONCEPTS AND FACTS
Intermediate Level (Grades 3-5)

STATE-O
Subject Area: Social Studies

Format: Bingo (page 61)
Players: 2 to whole class

<u>Directions</u>: Caller reads some fact about a state. Players match with name of state on cards. For example:

<u>Caller reads</u>:
Pearl Harbor was attacked on December 7, 1941

<u>Player matches on card</u>:
Hawaii

<u>Variations</u>: Names of principle bodies of water are matched with categories of river, bay, ocean, sea, lake, etc. on cards.

SENTENCE RUMMY
Subject Area: Language Arts

Format: Card Game (page 64)
Players: 3 or 4

<u>Directions</u>: Players collect sentence cards that form sequences. For example:

<u>Possible sequence might include</u>:
Mary went to school.
Mary read with her teacher.
Mary ate her dinner.

<u>Variations</u>: Collect fact cards relating to a state or historical figure.

INVENTOR CHECKERS
Subject Area: Social Studies

Format: Checkers (page 74)
Players: two

<u>Directions</u>: With each turn a player reads the name of an inventor on a task card and then names the major invention of that person. For example:

<u>Task Card</u>:
Howe
George Washington Carver

<u>Player may say</u>:
spinning jenny
peanut butter

<u>Variations</u>: Use American figures and important political events.

Games As Learning Tools

ANIMAL CATEGORIES Format: Concentration (page 78)
Subject Area: Science Players: 2 to whole class

Directions: Players read and match names of two of the same animal types and classify them as mammals, insects, fish. For example:

Appropriate matches might include:
  whale — elephant (mammals)
  trout — herring (fish)

Variations: Use different types of plants or rocks.

MULTIPLICATION DOMINOES Format: Dominoes (page 81)
Subject Area: Math Players: 2 to 4

Directions: Players match dominoes that equal the same amount. For example:

Appropriate matches might include:
  6 x 2 — 3 x 4 = 12
  10 x 4 — 8 x 5 = 40

Variations: Match addition, subtraction, division facts.

(Use any board game) Format: Board Game (page 85)
Subject Area: Language Arts Players: 2 to whole class

Directions: Players must answer a question correctly about an accompanying medicine label. If correct, the players advance. For example:

Task Card: Player may say:

| BUFFO |
| Take 3 times a day |
| for headaches. |
| Q. How often should |
| you take BUFFO? |

A. every four hours

Variations: Identify famous American figures in politics, sports, music, etc.

Game Ideas

CALL FACT[6]
Subject Area: Math

Format: Circle Game

Directions: Students stand in a circle. Each player is assigned a number. The Caller stands in the center holding a ball. The Caller says a number and throws the ball in the air. The player with that number must call out a math fact which has that number as an answer and catch the ball after it has bounced only once. For example: 10 is called. The player with 10 can say "2 x 5," "4 + 6," "20 ÷ 2," "14 — 4," or any other fact. The teacher may want to restrict the game to a specific operation such as only subtraction, addition, etc. Students may exchange numbers during the game. A player earns a point for each correct response. The player with the most points wins.

BANKER AND THE COINS[7]
Subject Area: Math

Format: Relay Game

Directions: Students form two teams. Each team member wears a sign denoting five cents, ten cents, quarters, fifty-cent pieces, dimes, nickels, and pennies. The teams line up facing each other with one half of the center space designated as each team's bank. For example:

Team A   x x x x x   x x x x x x x x

    (Team A Bank)   (Team B Bank)

Team B   x x x x x   x x x x x x x x

The Banker calls any amount of money up to the highest amount that can be made by the teams. At a given signal, each team tries to be the first to group themselves in their bank showing the correct amount. The group calls "In the Bank" and, if correct, they get one point. The winner is the team with the highest number of points.

---

[6]Ibid. pp. 60-61. (An adaptation of Call Blend)
[7]Ibid. pp. 143-144. (Adapted)

Games As Learning Tools

CONCEPTS AND FACTS
Middle Level (Grades 6-8)

GUESS WHO
Subject Area: Social Studies
Format: Bingo (page 61)
Players: 2 to whole class

<u>Directions</u>: Caller describes significant event. Players match with famous Americans on their cards. For example:

<u>Caller reads</u>:
    Organized Underground Railroad
    Unionized migrant workers

<u>Player matches on card</u>:
    Harriet Tubman
    Cesar Chavez

<u>Variations</u>: Use world leaders; leaders in science; the arts; sports.

LE BAG
Subject Area: Foreign Language
Format: Card Game (page 70)
Players: 2 to 4

<u>Directions</u>: Players collect matching pairs of equivalencies. For example:

<u>Possible matches might include</u>:
    amour - love   vous aimez - you love
    j'aime - I love

<u>Variations</u>: Artists and their works; elements in chemical compounds.

WHAT'S THE PLACE?
Subject Area: Social Studies
Format: Checkers (page 74)
Players: two

<u>Directions</u>: With each turn a player names the appropriate city, state, or country for the given task. For example:

<u>Task Card</u>:
  (capital) New Jersey
  (state) Albany

<u>Player may say</u>:
  Trenton
  New York

Game Ideas

LEAF LOOK
Subject Area: Science
Format: Concentration (page 78)
Players: 2 to whole class

Directions: Players match picture with name of leaf or tree. For example:

Appropriate matches might include:

oak — 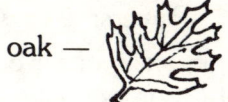   elm —

Variations: Match Indian tribes and nations; plants; trees; flowers.

DATE-MATCH
Subject Area: Social Studies
Format: Dominoes (page 81)
Players: 2 to 4

Directions: Players match dates of major significance with the events. For example:

Appropriate matches might include:
June 6, 1945 — D Day
1861-1865 — Civil War

Variations: Match world religions with deities; countries and continents.

(Use any board game)
Subject Area: Language Arts
Format: Board Game (page 85)
Players: 2 to 4

Directions: Players read sentence on task card and identify its structure. If correct, the player advances. For example:

Task Card:
The girl went shopping.
The girls ran into the building and told their teacher that a big dog was on the playground.

Player may say:
(reads sentence) — simple sentence
(reads sentence) — compound — complex sentence

Variations: Identify country of custom described on task card; identify branches of government responsible for specific government operations.

Games As Learning Tools

CONCEPTS AND FACTS
Senior Level (Grades 9-12)

JOB HUNT Format: Bingo (page 61)
Subject Area: Language Arts Players: 2 to whole class

<u>Directions</u>: Caller reads description of job skills of an occupation. Players match with occupation on card. For example:

<u>Caller reads</u>: <u>Player matches on card</u>:
Locates, studies fossils paleontologist
Runs switchboard PBX operator

<u>Variations</u>: Match government agency function with agency names.

KNOW YOUR ART Format: Card Game (page 69)
Subject Area: Art Players: 2 to 4

<u>Directions</u>: Using the *Go Fish* format, players categorize painters by their school. For example:

<u>Possible categories might include</u>:
French Impressionists: Monet, Renoir, Degas
Dutch: Rembrandt, Hals, Vermeer

<u>Variations</u>: Categorize authors and titles by types of literature.

LIT FACTS Format: Checkers (page 74)
Subject Area: English Literature Players: two

<u>Directions</u>: With each turn a player reads a quotation and identifies the correct character and/or play. For example:

<u>Task Card</u>: <u>Player may say</u>:
"To be, or not to be ..." Hamlet

<u>Variations</u>: In geology, identify classification categories of rocks; in chemistry, identify the reaction when two elements are combined.

Game Ideas

LEADERS Format: Concentration (page 78)
Subject Area: Social Studies Players: 2 to whole class

Directions: Players match world leader with country. For example:

Appropriate matches might include:
Ghandi — India
Franco — Spain

Variations: In African history, match old country name with new; in science match theory with theoretician (relativity/Einstein).

ANATOMY DOMINOES Format: Dominoes (page 81)
Subject Area: Science Players: 2 to 4

Directions: Players match parts of the body with their functions. For example:

Appropriate matches might include:
cerebellum — balance
kidney — "purify" blood

Variations: Match food source with vitamins and nutrients.

(Use any board game) Format: Board Game (page 85)
Subject Area: Math Players: 2 to 6

Directions: Players must solve algebraic equation on task cards. They can move 3 additional spaces if they can give the correct answer in less than 15 seconds. For example:

$4 + X - 3 = 10 - 2 \qquad X = \underline{\qquad}$

Variations: Identify function of underlined words in sentences; given a situation, identify the operating economic principle.

Games As Learning Tools

WORD ANALYSIS

Game Title	Game Format (A — active)	Subject Area*	Game Descr.	Guide- lines
PRIMARY LEVEL (GRADES K-2)				
Rhyme Word	Bingo	Lang. Arts	p. 121	p. 61
Phonic Fish	Card Game	Lang. Arts	p. 121	p. 69
Checker Blends	Checkers	Lang. Arts	p. 121	p. 74
Blend Search	Concentration	Lang. Arts	p. 122	p. 78
End Sound	Dominoes	Lang. Arts	p. 122	p. 81
(medial vowels)	Board Game	Lang. Arts	p. 122	p. 85
Match The Sound	Circle Game — A	Lang. Arts	p. 123	p. 91
See The Same	Relay Game — A	Lang. Arts	p. 123	p. 91
Blend Tag	Tag Game — A	Lang. Arts	p. 123	p. 91
INTERMEDIATE LEVEL (GRADES 3-5)				
Syllable Count	Bingo	Lang. Arts	p. 124	p. 61
Syllabico	Card Game	Lang. Arts	p. 124	p. 65
Add-N-Affix	Checkers	Lang. Arts	p. 124	p. 74
Ending Concentration	Concentration	Lang. Arts	p. 125	p. 78
Word Attack Dominoes	Dominoes	Any Subject	p. 125	p. 81
(roots and affixes)	Board Game	Lang. Arts	p. 125	p. 85
Syllables In A Basket	Circle Game — A	Lang. Arts	p. 126	p. 91
Letter Pattern Change	Relay Game — A	Lang. Arts	p. 126	p. 91
MIDDLE LEVEL (GRADES 6-8)				
Verb Find	Bingo	Foreign Lang.	p. 127	p. 61
Seven Card Up	Card Game	Lang. Arts	p. 127	p. 66
Syllable Checkers	Checkers	Lang. Arts	p. 128	p. 74
Roots and Prefixes	Concentration	Lang. Arts	p. 128	p. 78
Divide-A-Word	Dominoes	Lang. Arts	p. 128	p. 81
(conjugation)	Board Game	Foreign Lang.	p. 129	p. 85
SENIOR LEVEL (GRADES 9-12)				
Mystery Letter	Bingo	Lang. Arts	p. 129	p. 61
Syllabico	Card Game	Any Subject	p. 129	p. 65
Verbe Checkers	Checkers	Foreign Lang.	p. 130	p. 74
Dicto-Mark	Concentration	Lang. Arts	p. 130	p. 78
Equal Syllables	Dominoes	Any Subject	p. 130	p. 81
(dictionary)	Board Game	Lang. Arts	p. 131	p. 85

*Although examples are described in terms of specific subject area, variations are also included.

Game Ideas

WORD ANALYSIS
Primary Level (Grades K-2)

RHYME WORD
Subject Area: Language Arts

Format: Bingo (page 61)
Players: 2 to whole class

<u>Directions</u>: Caller reads words. Players identify words that rhyme on their cards. For example:

<u>Caller reads</u>:	<u>Player matches on card</u>:
cloud	loud
run	sun

<u>Variations</u>: Words are matched with any word analysis element.

PHONIC FISH
Subject Area: Language Arts

Format: Card Game (page 69)
Players: two

<u>Directions</u>: Using the *Go Fish* format, players collect picture (or word) cards that match certain phonic rules. For example: "Do you have a picture that begins like *boy*?"

<u>Variations</u>: Use words from experience stories, basals, or spelling lists.

CHECKER BLENDS
Subject Area: Language Arts

Format: Checkers (page 74)
Players: two

<u>Directions</u>: With each turn a player must identify a blend and give another word that begins with the same blend, using both words in sentences. For example:

Task Card:
    glad (word)
    truck (word)

Player may say:
    "glad: I am *glad* to be here."
    "glove: That is my *glove*."
    "truck: The *truck* was very big."
    "trout: I caught a *trout*."

<u>Variations</u>: Use any word analysis element with words or pictures.

Games As Learning Tools

BLEND SEARCH Format: Concentration (page 78)
Subject Area: Language Arts Players: 2 to whole class

<u>Directions</u>: Players must read and match words that begin with the same blend. For example:

<u>Appropriate matches might include</u>:
blank — blue
clam — class

<u>Variations</u>: Use any word analysis element with words.

END SOUND Format: Dominoes (page 81)
Subject Area: Language Arts Players: 2 to 4

<u>Directions</u>: Players match pictures with the same final consonant sound. For example:

<u>Appropriate matches might include</u>:
hat — goat
bag — rug

<u>Variations</u>: Use any word analysis element with words.

(Use any board game) Format: Board Game (page 85)
Subject Area: Language Arts Players: 2 to 4

<u>Directions</u>: Players must give a word with the same medial vowel sound as the word on the task card. They must then put their word into a sentence before advancing around the board. For example:

<u>Task Card</u>: <u>Player may say</u>:
cat "bat"; "I hit a baseball with a bat."

<u>Variations</u>: Use any word analysis element with words.

Game Ideas

MATCH THE SOUND[8]
Subject Area: Language Arts   Format: Circle Game

Directions: Students form a circle. At a given signal the players skip around in the circle until the Caller says "Stop." The Caller then says a word and throws the ball to one of the players. The player must catch the ball and say another word that begins with the same sound before the Caller counts to ten. The player scores a point if a correct word is given. Play continues in the same manner. The player with the most points wins. Other skills used could be final consonants, blends, vowels, digraphs, etc.

SEE THE SAME [9]
Subject Area: Language Arts   Format: Relay Game

Directions: Students are divided into two teams. Each team is provided with a box containing duplicate word cards, according to the skill being reinforced. The teams stand in rows behind a starting line. At a signal, the first player on each team runs to the box and tries to find two cards that have words with the same word analysis element in them. The first player to find two alike scores a point for his or her team. For example, with long vowels, a player would look for two words with the same long vowel, [bake] and [play] . Or, if stressing vowel patterns, a player would look for two words with the same pattern, [bake] [crate] or [moat] and [load] . Play continues in the same manner with the second player on each team. The team with the most points wins.

BLEND TAG
Subject Area: Language Arts   Format: Tag Game

Directions: Players stand facing each other in two lines. Each player wears a card with a consonant blend written on it. There must be duplicate sets of blend cards for each line. There may be more than one card for a given blend in the sets. The Caller either calls out or holds up a word card with a beginning blend. Those players having that blend run to change places before the Caller can tag them. A point is earned if a player is tagged. The player with the lowest score wins.

---

[8]Ibid. p. 59 (Adapted)
[9]Ibid. pp. 66-67. (Adapted)

Games As Learning Tools

WORD ANALYSIS
Intermediate Level (Grades 3-5)

SYLLABLE COUNT   Format: Bingo (page 61)
Subject Area: Language Arts   Players: 2 to whole class

Directions: The Caller reads words from one to five syllables. Players match with correct number on their card. For example:

    Caller reads: Player matches on card:
      procrastinate   4

Variations: Use words from subject-area units and basal readers.

SYLLABICO   Format: Card Game (page 65)
Subject Area: Language Arts   Players: 3 or 4

Directions: Using the *Syllabico* variation of rummy, players form words from syllable-unit cards. For example: [go] [ing] ; [farm] [er]

Variations: Use words from spelling, subject-area units.

ADD-N-AFFIX   Format: Checkers (page 74)
Subject Area: Language Arts   Players: two

Directions: With each turn, a player must read the root word on a task card, add an affix to the root and use the new word in a sentence. For example:

    Task Card: Player may say:
      appoint   disappoint; "He will try not to disappoint her."

Variations: Use words from spelling, subject-area units, basals.

Game Ideas

ENDING CONCENTRATION Format: Concentration (page 78)
Subject Area: Language Arts   Players: 2 to whole class

<u>Directions</u>: Players read and match two words that have the same endings. For example:

<u>Appropriate matches might include</u>:
    refrigerators — cars   harder — faster
    watched — talked   schools' — cooks'

<u>Variations</u>: Use words from spelling, subject-area units, basals.

WORD ATTACK DOMINOES Format: Dominoes (page 81)
Subject Area: Any Subject   Players: 2 to 4

<u>Directions</u>: Players match words that can be placed in the same category relating to some word analysis element. For example:

<u>Appropriate matches might include</u>:
    slipper — slow (initial consonant blend)
    gate — mode (final 'e' word)

<u>Variations</u>: Use words from spelling, subject-area units, basals.

(Use any board game) Format: Board Game (page 85)
Subject Area: Language Arts   Players: 2 to 4

<u>Directions</u>: Players add appropriate affixes to designated root words in a sentence on task cards. If correct, the players advance. For example:

<u>Task Card</u>:   <u>Player may say</u>:
I feel (comfort) when speaking "uncomfortable"
in front of this hostile group.

<u>Variations</u>: Use words from spelling, subject-area units, basals.

Games As Learning Tools

SYLLABLES IN A BASKET[10]   Format: Circle Game
Subject Area: Language Arts

Directions: The players form a circle and count off by twos. This means that alternating players in the circle are on team one while the others are on team two. The players remain in a single circle. Each team has a scorekeeper. A wastebasket is placed in the center of the circle. The Caller calls a word with any number of syllables and a beanbag is started around the circle. Each player must say a word with the same number of syllables and toss the beanbag into the basket. One point is scored for a correct word and one point for an accurate throw. Points are assigned to the team on which the player belongs. The team with the highest points is the winner.

LETTER PATTERN CHANGE [11]   Format: Relay Game
Subject Area: Language Arts

Directions: Two teams are formed but may remain in their seats. Cards with single-syllable words having an open, closed, or final 'e' vowel pattern are given to each player. The chalkboard is divided into two sections, one for each team. A word card is held up for the players to see. The player on each team who has that pattern with the same sounded vowel runs to the board, writes another word with the same pattern and vowel sound, and then returns to his or her seat. Each player is called on to read the word and name the letter pattern. For example, the word make is held up. A player holding the word grade runs to the board and writes the word "made." The player reads "made" and identifies it as final 'e' vowel-pattern word. A point is scored for each correct word written and for vowel pattern identification. The team with the most points is the winner. Word cards should be changed frequently among the players.

---

[10] Ibid. pp. 62-63. (An adaptation of Vowels In A Basket)
[11] Ibid. p. 69. (Adapted)

Game Ideas

WORD ANALYSIS
Middle Level (Grades 6-8)

VERB FIND
Subject Area: Foreign Language
Format: Bingo (page 61)
Players: 2 to whole class

<u>Directions</u>: Caller reads a verb. Players match with correct conjugation class on their cards. For example:

<u>Caller reads</u>:   <u>Player matches on card</u>:
allons   1st person plural, present tense

<u>Variations</u>: Use verbs from subject-area units and spelling lists.

SEVEN CARD UP
Subject Area: Language Arts
Format: Card Game (page 66)
Players: 2 to 4

<u>Directions</u>: Players form words using task cards with letters and letter combinations. Two-card words earn 5 points; three-card words earn 10 points; four-card words earn 15 points; five-card words earn 25 points. For example:

| g | r | a | d | e | = 25 points |

| gr | a | d | e | = 15 points |

| sl | i | d | ing | = 15 points |

<u>Variations</u>: Players make up words from spelling or subject-area lists.

SYLLABLE CHECKERS

Format: Checkers (page 74)
Subject Area: Language Arts
Players: two

Directions: With each turn a player must read a word on a task card, then pronounce it in syllables and identify the number of syllables in the word. For example:

<u>Task Card:</u>
   graduate
   willingness

<u>Player may say:</u>
   graduate; "grad-u-ate"; 3
   willingness; "will-ing-ness"; 3

Variations: Use words from spelling, subject-area units, and basals.

ROOTS AND PREFIXES

Format: Concentration (page 78)
Subject Area: Language Arts
Players: 2 to whole class

Directions: Players match root word with root and prefix and then identify the meanings of both words. For example:

Appropriate matches might include:
   happy — unhappy
   regard — disregard

Variations: Use words from spelling, subject-area units, and basals.

DIVIDE-A-WORD

Format: Dominoes (page 81)
Subject Area: Language Arts
Players: 2 to 4

Directions: Players match consonant-vowel patterns with words of the same pattern. For example:

Appropriate matches might include:
   vccv — pencil   vcv — acorn

Variations: Use words from spelling, subject-area units, and basals.

(Use any board game)　　　　　Format: Board Game (page 85)
Subject Area: Foreign Language　　　Players: 2 to 4

Directions: Players insert proper word form in the sentence on the task cards. If correct, the players advance. For example:

> Task Card:　　　　　　　Player may say:
> Je (être) près de la porte.　Je suis près de la porte.

Variations: Use cloze technique with foreign or English sentences.

WORD ANALYSIS
Senior Level (Grades 9-12)

MYSTERY LETTER　　　　　　Format: Bingo (page 61)
Subject Area: Language Arts　　　Players: 2 to whole class

Directions: Caller gives an identifying number and reads a spelling word with one letter deleted. Players match with missing letter on their cards and write the identifying number in that square. For example:

> Caller reads:　　　　　　　　　Player matches on card:
> "No. 1 — bureaucracy"　　　　"U" on board and writes
> "b-u-r-e-a-blank-c-r-a-c-y"　　1. in the square
> "Our government has
> 　become an unwieldy
> 　bureaucracy."

Variations: Use words from subject-area units.

SYLLABICO　　　　　　　　　Format: Card Game (page 65)
Subject Area: Any Subject　　　　Players: 3 or 4

Directions: Using the *Syllabication* variation of rummy, players form words from syllable-unit cards. For example: [bliss] [ful] [ly]

Variations: Use words from subject-area units.

Games As Learning Tools

VERBE CHECKERS Format: Checkers (page 74)
Subject Area: Foreign Language Players: two

Directions: With each turn a player must give the appropriate word form as designated on a task card. For example:

> Task Card: Player may say:
> 3rd person sing. of venir   Il vient

Variations: Identify origins of words from subject-area units. For example: aegis: Greek.

DICTO-MARK Format: Concentration (page 78)
Subject Area: Language Arts Players: 2 to whole class

Directions: Players match word with diacritical markings. For example:

> Appropriate matches might include:
> irreplaceable — ir — i — ˋplā — sə — bəl

Variations: Use words from subject-area units and basals.

EQUAL SYLLABLES Format: Dominoes (page 81)
Subject Area: Any Subject Players: 2 to 4

Directions: Players match words with similar number of syllables. Players must read each word that they match. For example:

> Appropriate matches might include:
> filibuster — democracy
> federal — democrat

Variations: Use words from spelling, subject-area units, and basals.

Game Ideas

(Use any board game)　　　　Format: Board Game (page 85)
Subject Area: Language Arts　　　　　　　　Players: 2 to 6

Directions: Players must place words in sequence on a task card according to alphabetical order within a timed period. If correct, the players may advance around the board. For example:

<u>Task Card</u>:　　　　　　<u>Player may say</u>:
reservoir, restaurant,　　remember, research, reserve,
remember, reserve　　　reservoir, restaurant
research,

Variations: Use one or more letters in words for alphabetizing.

Games As Learning Tools

GRAPHIC — SYMBOLIC

Game Title	Game Format (A — active)	Subject Area*	Game Descr.	Guide-lines
PRIMARY LEVEL (GRADES K-2)				
Math-O	Bingo	Math.	p. 133	p. 61
Alphabet Rummy	Card Game	Lang. Arts	p. 133	p. 64
Alphabet Checkers	Checkers	Lang. Arts	p. 133	p. 74
Weather-Watch	Concentration	Science	p. 134	p. 78
Tell-Time	Dominoes	Math.	p. 134	p. 81
(traffic signs)	Board Game	Lang. Arts	p. 134	p. 85
Rainbow	Circle Game — A	Lang. Arts	p. 135	p. 91
Shape Relay	Relay Game — A	Math.	p. 135	p. 91
Alphabet Tag	Tag Game — A	Lang. Arts	p. 136	p. 91
INTERMEDIATE LEVEL (GRADES 3-5)				
Music Notes	Bingo	Music	p. 136	p. 61
Measure Rummy	Card Game	Math.	p. 136	p. 64
House Hunt	Checkers	Soc. Studies	p. 137	p. 74
Geo Term	Concentration	Math.	p. 137	p. 78
Map Signs	Dominoes	Soc. Studies	p. 137	p. 81
(punctuation marks)	Board Game	Lang. Arts	p. 137	p. 85
What-Is-It Relay	Relay Game — A	Science	p. 138	p. 91
MIDDLE LEVEL (GRADES 6-8)				
Brev-O	Bingo	Lang. Arts	p. 138	p. 61
Cycle Rummy	Card Game	Math.	p. 139	p. 64
Map Hunt	Checkers	Soc. Studies	p. 139	p. 74
Dimensions	Concentration	Math.	p. 139	p. 78
Le Symbol	Dominoes	Foreign Lang.	p. 140	p. 81
(measurement)	Board Game	Home Econ.	p. 140	p. 85
SENIOR LEVEL (GRADES 9-12)				
Symb-O	Bingo	Bus. Educ.	p. 140	p. 61
Ad Match, or Le Bag	Card Game	Lang. Arts	p. 141	p. 65
Safe Driving	Checkers	Drivers' Ed.	p. 141	p. 74
Stitch and Sew	Concentration	Home Econ.	p. 141	p. 78
Chem Facts	Dominoes	Chemistry	p. 142	p. 81
(referee signals)	Board Game	Phys. Educ.	p. 142	p. 85

*Although examples are described in terms of specific subject area, variations are also included.

Game Ideas

GRAPHIC-SYMBOLIC
Primary Level (Grades K-2)

MATH-O
Subject Area: Math

Format: Bingo (page 61)
Players: 2 to whole class

Directions: Caller reads a "set" description. Players match with appropriate numeral on their cards. For example:

Caller reads:	Player matches on card:
2 sets of ten	20

Variations: Match pictures to make compound words.

ALPHABET RUMMY
Subject Area: Language Arts

Format: Card Game (page 64)
Players: 2 to 4

Directions: Using the *Rummy* format, players match uppercase and lowercase letters of the alphabet. For example:

Appropriate matches might include:
- B — b   b — b
- C — c   F — F

Variations: Match number words or sets of objects with numerals.

ALPHABET CHECKERS
Subject Area: Language Arts

Format: Checkers (page 74)
Players: two

Directions: With each turn a player must identify the letter which occurs alphabetically before or after the letter on the checker that the player moves. For example:

Letter on checker to be moved:	Player may say:
t	"s" or "u"
k	"j" or "l"

Variations: Put letter into a three-letter sequence.

Games As Learning Tools

WEATHER-WATCH Format: Concentration (page 78)
Subject Area: Science Players: 2 to whole class

<u>Directions</u>: Players match two related weather pictures. For example:

<u>Appropriate matches might include:</u>
pictures of: umbrella — rain sled — snow

<u>Variations</u>: Match pictures relating to home, school, work, play, etc.

TELL-TIME Format: Dominoes (page 81)
Subject Area: Math Players: 2 to 4

<u>Directions</u>: Players match clock faces with written time. For example:

Appropriate matches might include:

— 3:00 p.m.

<u>Variations</u>: Match coins and their values; street signs.

(Use any board game) Format: Board Game (page 85)
Subject Area: Language Arts Players: 2 to 4

<u>Directions</u>: Players must identify a traffic sign on a task card and tell what they would do when they see that sign. If correct, players advance around the board. For example:

Task Card: Player may say:

"Stop Sign: I would look both ways to make sure the cars were not coming before I crossed the street."

<u>Variations</u>: Identify values of coins.

Game Ideas

RAINBOW Format: Circle Game
Subject Area: Language Arts

<u>Directions</u>: The players form a circle facing center. The Caller stands in the center. Each player wears a paper-chain necklace of a certain color. The Caller names a color and all children wearing that color run to change places while the Caller tries to get one of the spaces left open by the running children. The player who does not get one of the spaces becomes the next Caller. The Caller may call "Rainbow" and then all players must change places. The Caller may hold up objects for visual recognition of colors.

SHAPE RELAY[12] Format: Relay Game
Subject Area: Math

<u>Directions</u>: Two flat, wide boxes are placed about ten feet away from two teams of players. In the boxes are objects of various shapes such as small boxes (squares or rectangles), bottle caps, triangles, (musical instruments), triangular party hats, knitted caps, small milk cartons, etc. The Leader holds up a cardboard shape. At a given signal, the first player on each team runs to his or her box and takes out as many objects with the indicated shape as can be found while the Leader counts to five. A point is scored for every object having the correct shape. An object is counted correct even though only part of it may have the designated shape. For example:

The top of the milk carton would get a point if the shape designated was a triangle. The bottom of the carton would get a point if the shape shown was a rectangle. The player must identify what part of the object is the shape designated to score a point. The team with the most points is the winner.

---

[12]Ibid. pp. 82-83. (Adapted)

ALPHABET TAG

Format: Tag Game

Subject Area: Language Arts

Directions: Players stand facing each other in two lines. Each player wears a card with a letter of the alphabet in either uppercase or lowercase. The alphabet cards are intermixed, making sure that the uppercase and lowercase of any one letter are not on the same side or in the same order. The Caller calls out a letter and the players with that letter (uppercase or lowercase) run to change places before the Caller can tag them. Any player caught scores a point and becomes Caller. The player with the fewest points wins the game. This game may also be played with number words and numerals.

GRAPHIC-SYMBOLIC
Intermediate Level (Grades 3-5)

MUSIC NOTES

Format: Bingo (page 61)

Subject Area: Music

Players: 2 to whole class

Directions: The Caller reads names of musical symbols. Players match with correct symbols on their cards. For example:

Caller reads:	Player matches on card:
quarter note	♩
treble clef	

Variations: Match map symbols with what they represent.

MEASURE RUMMY

Format: Card Game (page 64)

Subject Area: Math

Players: 3 or 4

Directions: Using the *Rummy* format, players collect cards with the same category of measurement terms (dry, liquid, linear, etc.). For example:

| 4 pints | 1 quart | 3 gallons | = | 1 liquid set |

Variations: Players may form sets with equal numerical sentences. For example:

| 5 + 3 | 4 x 2 | 8 − 0 | = | 1 set |

Game Ideas

HOUSE HUNT
Subject Area: Social Studies

Format: Checkers (page 74)
Players: two

Directions: With each turn a player must identify the type of house on a task card and tell the country of its origin. For example:

Task Card:

Player may say:
"chalet, a house in Switzerland"

Variations: Identify map symbols on task cards.

GEO TERM
Subject Area: Math

Format: Concentration (page 78)
Players: 2 to whole class

Directions: Players match geometric shapes with terms. For example:

Appropriate matches might include:

☐ — square   △ — triangle   ▱ — cube

Variations: Match words with abbreviations.

MAP SIGNS
Subject Area: Social Studies

Format: Dominoes (page 81)
Players: 2 to 4

Directions: Players match map symbols with their meanings. For example:

Appropriate matches might include:

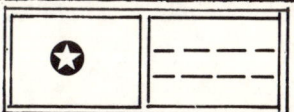

Variations: Match weather map symbols.

(Use any board game)
Subject Area: Language Arts

Format: Board Game (page 85)
Players: 2 to 4

Directions: Players read sentences on task cards with correct intonation according to the punctuation. If correct, players advance. For example:

Task Cards:
Oh, no? Oh, no!

Players must:
Use correct intonation.

Variations: Identify Safety Patrol or bicycle hand signals on task cards.

Games As Learning Tools

WHAT-IS-IT RELAY
Format: Relay Game
Subject Area: Science

Directions: Duplicate pictures related to a science unit on weather are placed along a chalkboard ledge. Two teams are designated and stand in rows ten to fifteen feet from the board. Each team is assigned one half of the board and a set of pictures of cloud formations and other weather conditions. The Caller describes one of the pictures. At the signal "Go" the first player on each team runs to the board and selects the picture described by the Caller. One point is scored for the team whose player first identifies the correct picture. For example, the Caller says "A nimbus cloud. Go." Players would race to the board and select a picture of a nimbus cloud formation. Play continues in the same manner with each team member. The team with the most points wins.

GRAPHIC-SYMBOLIC
Middle Level (Grades 6-8)

BREV-O
Format: Bingo (page 61)
Subject Area: Language Arts
Players: 2 to whole class

Directions: Caller reads a word from catalogues, bus schedules, phone book. Players match with abbreviations and/or symbols on their cards. For example:

Caller reads:	Player matches on card:
milligram	mg (symbol)
recommended daily requirement	RDA (abbreviation)

Variations: Use symbols and abbreviations in sport pages, recipes.

Game Ideas

CYCLE RUMMY Format: Card Game (page 64)
Subject Area: Math Players: 2 to 4

Directions: Players collect growth sequences of plants and animals from pictures on cards. For example:

An appropriate sequence might be:

pictures of: caterpillar   chrysallis   butterfly

Variations: Sequence cartoon without words or with words deleted.

MAP HUNT Format: Checkers (page 74)
Subject Area: Social Studies Players: two

Directions: With each turn a player must identify map symbols on the task card. For example:

Task Card: Player may say:

route symbol for interstate highway

state capitol

Variations: Use symbols and abbreviations from functional reading situations.

DIMENSIONS Format: Concentration (page 78)
Subject Area: Math Players: 2 to whole class

Directions: Players match dimensions with geometric shapes. For example:

Appropriate matches might include:

4 x 4 x 4 — equilateral triangle
5 x 5 x 6 x 4 — trapezoid

Variations: Use symbols and abbreviations from functional reading situations.

Games As Learning Tools

LE SYMBOL Format: Dominoes (page 81)
Subject Area: Foreign Language Players: 2 to 4

<u>Directions</u>: Players match symbols with foreign language words. For example:

<u>Appropriate matches might include</u>:
international road signs — el hospital, el telefono

<u>Variations</u>: Use English words and match with international road signs.

(Use any board game) Format: Board Game (page 85)
Subject Area: Home Economics Players: 2 to 4

<u>Directions</u>: Players must identify measurement abbreviations on task cards before advancing around the board. For example:

<u>Task Card:</u>	<u>Player may say:</u>
T.	tablespoon
oz.	ounce

<u>Variations</u>: Identify science and math symbols and abbreviations.

GRAPHIC-SYMBOLIC
Senior Level (Grades 9-12)

SYMB-O Format: Bingo (page 61)
Subject Area: Business Education Players: 2 to whole class

<u>Directions</u>: The Caller reads a word. Players match with shorthand symbol on their cards. For example:

<u>Caller reads:</u>	<u>Player matches on card:</u>
dear	↱

<u>Variations</u>: Identify science abbreviations.

Game Ideas

AD MATCH or LE BAG   Format: Card Game (page 65)
Subject Area: Language Arts   Players: 2 (Ad Match) or 4 (Le Bag)

<u>Directions</u>: Players form sets of cards that match newspaper classified advertisement abbreviations with their meanings. For example:

<u>Appropriate matches might include:</u>

p/t — part-time	br. — bedroom
min. — minimum	EOE — Equal Opportunity Employer

<u>Variations</u>: Use abbreviations from amusement or financial pages.

SAFE DRIVING   Format: Checkers (page 74)
Subject Area: Drivers' Education   Players: two

<u>Directions</u>: Players must identify highway traffic signs on task cards and tell what they mean to drivers. For example:

<u>Task Card</u>:

<u>Player may say</u>:

Caution; slow down; a steep hill ahead

<u>Variations</u>: Identify chemical formulas and compounds.

STITCH AND SEW   Format: Concentration (page 78)
Subject Area: Home Economics   Players: 2 to whole class

<u>Directions</u>: Players match pattern symbols with directions. For example:

<u>Appropriate matches might include:</u>

)>> — dart   ←——→ — lengthwise of goods

<u>Variations</u>: Use music symbols and terminology.

Games As Learning Tools

CHEM FACTS Format: Dominoes (page 81)
Subject Area: Chemistry Players: 2 to 4

<u>Directions</u>: Players match chemical formulas with names. For example:

<u>Appropriate matches might include</u>:

CO_2 — carbon dioxide; H_2SO_4 — sulphuric acid

<u>Variations</u>: Identify physics formulas.

(Use any board game) Format: Board Game (page 85)
Subject Area: Physical Education Players: 2 to 6

<u>Directions</u>: Players must identify referee signals from pictures on task cards. If correct, players may advance around the board.

<u>Variations</u>: Use referee signals for different sports.

Chapter 7

Other Sources For Game Ideas

The books selected for this bibliography comprise only some of the available materials on games for learning. It should be noted that the term "games" in these books is not necessarily synonymous with the authors' definition of games.

For your information, the books have been coded in the following manner to indicate the curriculum levels for which the material seems most appropriate: E — elementary   S — secondary
Although these books have been coded by grade level designation, it has been found that much of the elementary-level material can be used by middle and secondary school teachers working with remedial students.

Bentley, William G. <u>Indoor and Outdoor Games</u>. Belmont, California: Fearon Publishers, 1966. (E)
> Essentially a book of physical education and recreation games. There is a possibility of utilizing these ideas to design games incorporating academic skills.

Corle, Clyde G. <u>Skill Games for Mathematics</u>. Dansville, New York: The Instructor Publications, Inc., 1972. (E)
> Primary and intermediate games and activities are described in this publication. Ideas include active games, manipulative materials, paper and pencil activities, finger plays, and board games.

Crescimbeni, Joseph. <u>Arithmetic Enrichment Activities for Elementary School Children</u>. West Nyack, New York: Parker Publishing Co., 1965. (E)
> This book of activities is divided into six parts. One part deals exclusively with games. All of the games are competitive and include both active and passive games.

Games As Learning Tools

Criscuolo, Nicholas P. 100 <u>Individualized Activities for Reading</u>. Belmont, California: Fearon Publishers, 1974. (E)
    The activities in this book were designed for individual work. However, some of the ideas could be put into a game format for group use.

Daniels, Steven. <u>How 2 Gerbils, 20 Goldfish, 200 Games, 2000 Books and I Taught Them How to Read</u>. Philadelphia, Pennsylvania: The Westminster Press, 1971. (S)
    This book tells the story of one junior high school teacher's successful experiences in an "impossible" urban school. A major thrust of his program was the use of stimulating classroom games. The "how-to's" are carefully delineated.

Davis, Arnold R., and Donald C. Miller. <u>Science Games</u>. Belmont, California: Fearon Publishers, 1974. (E)
    This book contains games for primary and intermediate grades. Dominoes, bingo, tic-tac-toe, chalkboard, and oral games are included. Materials and preparation are kept at a minimum.

Dorsey, Mary E. <u>Reading Games and Activities</u>. Belmont, California: Fearon Publishers, 1972. (E)
    Games and activities in this book are organized according to a sequence of skills. Ideas for group games, independent activities, learning centers, puzzles, and oral activities are presented.

Forte, Imogene, Mary Ann Pangle, and Robbie Tupa. <u>Center Stuff for Nooks, Crannies, and Corners</u>. Nashville, Tennessee: Incentive Publications, Inc., 1974. (E)
    Most of the material in this book is specifically designed for learning centers. However, there are some game ideas incorporated into the learning center ideas. Additionally, there are worksheets and many independent activities. Games include active and card games.

Garrison, Evangeline L. <u>Individualized Reading</u>. Dansville, New York: The Instructor Publications, Inc., 1970. (E)
    The activities in this book are designed to be used independently. A few group activities are included and could be incorporated into games.

Other Sources For Game Ideas

Goodrich, Warren. <u>Learning About Science Through Games.</u> Harrisburg, Pennsylvania: Stackpole Books, 1964. (E)
> The activities in this book are of the active type and planned for whole class participation. Many of the activities are designed to be utilized out-of-doors. Some competitive games are included. The book provides good resource material.

Grant, Niels, Jr. <u>Word Games</u>. Belmont, California: Fearon Publishers, 1971. (E, S)
> The games in this book are all of the pencil and paper type and are more seatwork activities than games.

Herr, Selma E. <u>Learning Activities for Reading</u>. Dubuque, Iowa: Wm. C. Brown Publishers, 1977. (Second Edition). (E)
> This book is organized by skill areas. The author gives many suggestions for individualizing reading activities. Ideas for learning centers, games, and worksheets are presented with indications of grade level usage.

Humphrey, James H. and Dorothy D. Sullivan. <u>Teaching Slow Learners Through Active Games</u>. Springfield, Illinois: Charles C Thomas, Publisher, 1970. (E)
> Although this book was especially written for slow learners, it can be used by teachers of all students at the primary and intermediate levels. Over two hundred games are described in detail for developing and reinforcing reading, science, and math skills. The purposes of each game are outlined, and applications of the concepts inherent in the games are clearly explained. Adaptations for each game are included to provide broad use of the games.

Kaplan, Sandra Nina, Jo Ann Butom Kaplan, Sheila Kunishima Madsen, and Bettye K. Taylor. <u>Change for Children</u>. Pacific Palisades, California: Goodyear Publishing Company, Inc. (E)
> The authors present many ideas which can be used in learning centers for independent activities. Several ready-to-use learning center ideas are described in detail. Worksheets are included at the back of the book so that teachers may copy them for use in the centers. Each center idea has a section titled "Games and Activities." Some of the games are competitive and are both active and passive types.

Games As Learning Tools

Keith, Joy L. <u>Word Attack Joy</u>. Naperville, Illinois: Reading Joy, 1974. (E)
> This book is a potpourri of techniques for reinforcing word attack skills. Games, independent activities, mobiles, and puzzles are included. Some of the ideas are simple to execute, while others are fairly elaborate in terms of materials and design. Although many of the directions for playing and making the games are unclear, there are many useful ideas. Also included is some narrative on word attack as well as group and individual word attack tests.

Keith, Joy L. <u>Comprehension Joy</u>. Naperville, Illinois: Reading Joy, 1974. (E)
> <u>Comprehension Joy</u> appears to be more applicable to intermediate reading skills. The same types of activities included in <u>Work Attack Joy</u> reappear here. The general comments as to directions and materials are also true of this book. Narratives on comprehension skills, informal tests, and hints on game making are found at the beginning of the book. At the end of the book are reference word lists.

Landin, Leslie. <u>100 Blackboard Games</u>. Belmont, California: Fearon Publishers, 1956. (E)
> The only necessary tools for playing these games are a chalkboard and some chalk. The games actively involve students but some require a good bit of teacher preparation.

Lorton, Mary Baratta. <u>Workjobs</u>. Menlo Park, California: Addison-Wesley Publishing Company, 1972. (E)
> The activities in this book are designed for early childhood education. Most of the materials pictured are teacher-made and are manipulative in nature. The pictures and explanations are excellent.

Metzner, Seymour. <u>One-Minute Game Guide</u>. Belmont, California: Fearon Publishers, 1973. (E)
> Language arts and arithmetic chalkboard games are arranged in approximate order of difficulty. Very little or no preparation is needed to play. Most of the activities are teacher-directed; some of the games are self-competitive.

Other Sources for Game Ideas

Metzner, Seymour. <u>77 Games for Reading Groups</u>. Belmont, California: Fearon Publishers, 1973. (E)
>Ideas that are given for reading games require paper and pencils. Many of the activities involve students preparing their own materials and then using them in game situations. Both teacher-directed and student-directed games are included. All of the activities are designed for primary and intermediate grades.

Mulac, Margaret E. <u>Perceptual Games and Activities.</u> New York: Harper and Row, Publishers, 1977. (S and E)
>All the senses are utilized in these games and activities for learning skills. Content from the mathematics and science areas are emphasized. These games are oriented not only to the elementary grades but also have creative approaches to secondary context.

Musselman, Virginia W. <u>Learning About Nature Through Games</u>. Harrisburg, Pennsylvania: Stackpole Books, 1967. (E)
>The author defines games as having enjoyment as their basic ingredient. The games in this book are all designed for active involvement of the participants. Nature walks and experiments are some of the game activities. Puzzles, stunts, and board games are included. This book was primarily prepared for recreational situations but has good ideas for the classroom teacher.

Sharp, Richard M., Vicki F. Sharp, and Anita C. Solza. <u>30 Math Games for the Elementary Grades</u>. Belmont, California: Fearon Publishers, 1974. (E)
>This entire book is devoted to gameboard ideas. Directions are given for playing the games with accompanying diagrams of the boards. Many of the gameboard ideas could be redesigned for other curriculum areas.

Spache, Evelyn B. <u>Reading Activities for Child Involvement</u>. Boston: Allyn and Bacon, Inc., 1976 (Second Edition). (E)
>The author has described activities incorporating games, worksheets, learning centers, graphs, oral activities, and other techniques for reinforcing reading skills. Activities are arranged by skills and a cross-index is provided at the end of the book.

Games As Learning Tools

Spice Series. Stevensville, Michigan; Educational Service, Inc. (E)
>Twenty books written from 1960 to 1976 comprise this series. These books all give ideas for games, learning centers, worksheets, and independent activities. Areas covered include:

>Spice (primary language arts), 1960
>Probe (science), 1962
>Plus (mathematics), 1964
>Spark (social studies), 1965
>Create (art), 1966
>Action (physical education), 1967
>Stage (dramatics), 1968
>Rescue (remedial reading), 1970
>Anchor (intermed. lang. arts), 1970
>Pride (Black studies), 1971
>Launch (early learning), 1972
>Flair (creative writing), 1972
>Note (music), 1973
>Eco (ecology), 1974
>Choice (economic system), 1975
>Prevent (safety), 1975
>Challenge (intermed. math.), 1975
>Growth (elementary health), 1975
>Meter (metric system), 1975
>Inquire (intermediate science), 1976

Sullivan, Dorothy D. and James H. Humphrey. Teaching Reading Through Motor Learning. Springfield, Illinois: Charles C Thomas, Publishers, 1973. (E)
>Using active games as learning games in reading are thoroughly discussed by the authors in this book. Games are organized by skill areas with the concept, activity procedures, and application being given for each game. Use of games as diagnostic tools is presented in the final chapter.

Thomason, Mary E. Modern Math Games, Activities, and Puzzles. Belmont, California: Fearon Publishers, 1972. (E)
>Chapter one of this book deals with games. Techniques include flash cards, oral activities, bingo, checkers, dominoes, and one active game. The remaining two chapters are entirely concerned with puzzles and activities. Some of the ideas for activities could be incorporated into game formats.

Thompson, Richard A. Energizers for Reading Instruction. West Nyack, New York: Parker Publishing Co., 1973. (E)
>This book is divided into ten chapters which, the author suggests, follow the sequence of skills introduced in most reading programs. Games utilizing boards, cards, and manipulative objects are intermixed with individual and independent activities. The last chapter contains a list of sources for obtaining commercial reading games and activities.

Other Sources For Game Ideas

Wagner, Guy, Max Hosier, and Mildred Blackman. Listening Games. Darien, Connecticut: Teachers Publishing Corporation, 1962. (E)
>The activities in this book are designed to enhance students' listening skills. The book is divided into seven parts. Games are listed in order of increasing difficulty. Many of the activities require no preparation and are generally oral.

Wagner, Guy, and Max Hosier. Reading Games. Darien, Connecticut: Teachers Publishing Corporation, 1974 (Second Edition). (E)
>The organization of the material in this book is similar to that of the above book. Games include cards, checkers, pencil and paper activities, and bingo. Some of the activities are designed to be competitive while others are more independent exercises.

Waynant, Louise F., and Robert M. Wilson. Learning Centers . . . A Guide for Effective Use. Paoli, Pennsylvania: The Instructo Corporation, 1974. (S and E)
>The authors have presented with great clarity the procedures for developing learning centers and implementing their use as a viable part of the classroom curriculum. This book may be considered a companion piece of Games as Learning Tools and provides the descriptive detail necessary for the effective classroom use of learning centers.

Waynant, Louise F. Learning Centers II . . . Practical Ideas For You. Paoli, Pennsylvania: Instructo/McGraw-Hill. 1977. (S and E)
>This book focuses on the use of learning centers to meet individual needs. It is shown how learning centers can be used to expand the curriculum, to reinforce skills and concepts, to help students set realistic goals. While extensive learning center formats are presented, several chapters are devoted specifically to learning center ideas for exceptional students and intermediate students with reading difficulties. Many tips for constructing simple manipulative devices are included.

Games As Learning Tools

Games Index

Action Relay
  language arts, 101
Add-N-Affix
  checkers,
  language arts, 124
Ad Match
  cards,
  language arts, 141
Alphabet Checkers
  language arts, 133
Alphabet Rummy
  language arts, 133
Alphabet Tag
  language arts, 136
Anatomy Dominoes
  science, 119
Animal Bingo
  science, 110
Animal Categories
  concentration,
  science, 114
Auto Bingo
  industrial arts, 107
Banker and the Coins
  relay,
  mathematics, 115
Blend Search
  concentration,
  language arts, 122
Blend Tag
  language arts, 123

Board Games
English literature,
  Old English terms, 108
foreign language, 129
  conjugation, 130
home economics,
  measurement, 140
language arts,
  compound words, 100
  dictionary, 131
  medial vowels, 122
  medicine labels, 114
  punctuation, 137
  roots and affixes, 125
  sentence struc., 117
  traffic signs, 134
mathematics,
  alg. equations, 119
  coin values, 115
physical education,
  referee signals, 142
  sports terms, 103
social studies,
  geo. terms, 106
Brev-O
  bingo,
  language arts, 138
Call Fact
  circle,
  mathematics, 115
Category Rummy
  science, 105
Checkers, 44-45

Checker Blends
  language arts, 121
Chem Facts
  dominoes, 142
Clue Bingo
  language arts, 105
Color Match
  cards,
  language arts, 99
  concentration, 45-46
Cross the Bridge
  tag,
  language arts, 101
Cycle Rummy
  mathematics, 139
Date-Match
  dominoes,
  social studies, 117
Definition Dominoes
  any subject, 106
Dicto-Mark
  concentration,
  language arts, 130
Dimensions
  concentration,
  mathematics, 139
Divide-A-Word
  dominoes,
  language arts, 128
Dominoes, 46

End Sound
dominoes,
language arts, 122

Ending Concentration
language arts, 125

Equal Syllables
dominoes,
any subject, 130

Find-A-Word
stunt,
language arts, 104

Food-O-Dominoes
home economics, 108

Geo
concentration,
geometry, 108

Geo Term
concentration,
mathematics, 137

Give-the-Word Checkers
language arts, 99

Go Fish
cards, 118

Going Home
circle,
science, 112

Guess Who
bingo,
social studies, 116

History Poker
cards,
social studies, 107

Holiday Concentration
social studies, 111

House Hunt
checkers,
social studies, 137

Inventor Checkers
social studies, 113

Job Hunt
bingo,
language arts, 118

Know Your Art
cards, 118

Le Bag
cards, 70
foreign lang., 116

Le Symbol
dominoes,
language arts, 140

Leaders
concentration,
social studies, 119

Leaf Look
concentration,
science, 117

Letter Pattern Change
relay,
language arts, 126

Lit Facts
checkers,
English literature, 118

Magic "e" Dominoes
language arts, 100

Map Hunt
checkers,
social studies, 139

Map Signs
dominoes,
social studies, 137

Match
cards,
any subject, 65

Match the Sound
circle,
language arts, 123

Math-O
bingo, 133

Math Pairs
concentration, 100

Math Rummy, 110

Measure Match
concentration,
mathematics, 106

Measure Rummy
mathematics, 136

Multiplication Dominoes, 114

Music Notes
bingo, 136

Mystery Letter
bingo,
language arts, 129

Number Tag
mathematics, 113

Object Dominoes
language arts, 111

Opposites Bingo
language arts, 99

Opposites Concentration
language arts, 103

Pair of Blends Rummy, 49

Phonic Fish
cards, 121

Phrase Match
cards, 69
language arts, 102

Poker
seven-card stud, 66

Politico
checkers,
Am. Government, 107

Rainbow
circle,
language arts, 135

Rhyme Chase
circle,
language arts, 104

151

Games As Learning Tools

Rhyme Word
bingo,
language arts, 121

Roots and Prefixes
concentration,
language arts, 128

Rummy, 64-65

Safe Driving
checkers,
drivers' education, 141

See The Same
relay,
language arts, 123

Sentence Rummy
language arts, 113

Seven Card Up, 66
language arts, 127

Shape Relay
mathematics, 135

State-O
social studies, 113

Stitch and Sew
concentration,
home economics, 141

Syllabico
cards,
language arts, 124, 129

Syllable Checkers
language arts, 128

Syllable Count
bingo,
language arts, 124

Syllables In A Basket
circle,
language arts, 126

Symb-O
bingo,
business
education, 140

Tell-Time
dominoes,
mathematics, 134

Tracking Dinosaurs, 49-50

Time-Line Bingo
social studies, 102

Verbe Checkers
foreign languge, 130

Verb Find
bingo,
foreign language, 127

Weather Report
relay,
science, 112

Weather-Watch
concentration,
science, 134

Weather Word-O
checkers,
science, 102

What-Is-It-Relay
science, 138

What's The Number
checkers,
mathematics, 110

What's The Place
checkers,
social studies, 116

Word-Alike Dominoes
language arts, 103

Word Attack Dominoes
any subject, 125

Word Erase
relay,
social studies, 104

Words-In-A-Circle
language arts, 100

Word Wise
checkers,
foreign language, 105

Subject and Author Index

Active games, 2, 4-5, 90-93, 100-101, 104, 112-115, 123, 126, 135-136, 138

Adaptability of games, 8, 25-26, 44-46, 52-53, 62, 72, 74-75, 78, 81-82, 87, 90-92, 93-142
(*See also* Designing games)

Aides, 19
(*See also* Parents, helping games construction)

Answer keys, 76, 87

Assigning games, 17, 19

Attitudes
parents, 13-15
students, 15-16
teachers, 1, 7

Basic game guidelines (*See* Games, basic guidelines)

Bentley, William G., 143

Bilodeau, Edward A., 6, 12

Bilodeau, Ina, 6, 12

Bingo, 62-63; chart, 63

Blackman, Mildred, 149

Board games, 85-88; chart, 89

Card games, 64-72; chart, 73

Chance, element of, 2, 47-48, 76, 85-88

Checkers, 74-76; chart, 77

Circle games, 90-92; chart, 93

Coding system for game identification, 22-26

Commercial games, 1, 54-55
adapting to learning games, 54
use of old game parts, 55
competition, 2

Concentration, 78-79; chart, 80

Concepts and facts games, 110-119; chart, 109

Conferences, 8, 15-19, 27

Constructing games, 13-15
making adaptable, 52-56
using commercial games, 54-55
designing: getting started, 43-47
guidelines for, 47-52
making durable, 53
making storable, 53
workshops, 56-58

Content skills games
vocabulary, 95, 99-108; chart, 98
concepts and facts, 95, 110-119; chart, 109
word analysis, 95, 121-131; chart, 120
graphic-symbolic, 95, 133-142; chart, 132

Corle, Clyde, 143

Cross reference file system, 22-24

Criscuolo, Nicholas P., 144

Curriculum, supplementing the, 20-21

Daniels, Steven, 144

Davey, Beth, 12, 33

Davis, Arnold B., 144

Decision-making, 94

Definition of a game, 2

Denellen, Ogden, 44

Designing games (*see* Constructing games)

DeVries, D.L., 2, 12

Diagnosis, 1, 19-20, 31-40
definition, 31
why use games, 32
learning styles, 33

Games As Learning Tools

informal observation, 33-35
for objectives, 33-35
adapting tests, 35
record keeping, 37-40
self-evaluation, 9-11, 39-40

Dickerson, Dolores, 5, 12

Directions, 31, 48-50
(*See also* Games, directions for)

Dolinsky, Richard, 6, 12

Dominoes, 81-83; chart, 84

Dorsey, Mary E., 144

Durability of games, 61, 71, 74-75, 81-82, 88

Edwards, K.J., 2, 12

Evaluation
(*See also* Conferences)
of concepts or skills, 10-11
of directions for play, 10, 30
of game, 10, 30
student self-evaluation, 8-11, 15, 26-27, 39-40, 92
teacher evaluation, 8-9, 16-17, 31, 92

Formats
passive games, 61-89
active games, 90-93

Forte, Imogene, 144

Gambrell, Linda, 9, 12

Games
basic guidelines, 22, 47-52
active games, 90-92
bingo, 61-62
board games, 85-88
card games, 71-72
checkers, 74-76
concentration, 78-79
dominoes, 81-83
construction of, (*see* Constructing games)

curriculum
supplementing the, 20-21
integral part of, 7-8, 16-19
individualizing instruction, 7-9, 16-20
definition of, 2
designing games (*see* Constructing games)
for diagnosis, 1, 19-20, 31-40
directions for, 59
active games, 90
bingo, 61
board games, 85
card games, 64-70
checkers, 74
concentration, 78
dominoes, 81
evaluation, 8, 10-13, 26, 95
formats
bingo, 61-62; chart, 63
board games, 85-88; chart, 89
card games, 64-72; chart, 73
circle games, 90-92; chart, 93
checkers, 74-76; chart, 77
concentration, 78-79; chart, 80
dominoes, 81-83; chart, 84
relay games, 90-92; chart, 93
tag and other games, 90-92; chart, 93
independent activities, 8, 16-22
for individualizing instruction, 7-9, 16-20
management of, 21-30
coding system for game identification, 22-26
cross reference file system, 22-24
introducing games, 21-22
master file of games, 22-24
time schedules, 16-20
record keeping, 37-40
organizing for learning activities
as independent activities, 8, 16-18
teacher-directed, 18-20
supplementary activities, 20-21
peer learning, 2, 17-18, 29, 72
for reinforcement, 3, 5-6, 13-18, 20, 22

selection
 student self-selection, 8-10, 16, 20, 26-27
 teacher selection, 8-11, 16-19, 26-27, 94
storage, 53
student self-evaluation, 8-11, 26-27, 92
type of
 active, 4-5, 90-93, 100-101, 104, 112, 115, 123, 126, 135-136, 138
 passive, 3, 61-89
 simulation, 4

Games Skill Center, 25

Garrison, Evangeline L., 144

Getting started, 21-22, 41-48

Goodrich, Warren, 145

Grant, Niels, Jr., 145

Graphic-Symbolic games, 108, 133-142; chart, 132

Herr, Selma E., 145

Hosier, Max, 149

Humphrey, James H., 6, 7, 12, 32, 100-101, 145, 148

Ideas for games
 content skills by subject areas, Chapter 6, 95-142
 designing and making, Chapter 4, 41-58
 formats and directions, Chapter 5, 59-94

Independent use of games, 8, 16-18

Individualizing instruction, 7-9, 16-18, 62, 75

Introducing games, 21-22

Kaplan, Jo Ann B., 145

Kaplan, Sandra N., 145

Keith, Joy L., 146

Landin, Leslie, 146

Learning games, 2
 (*See also* Games)

Lorton, Mary B., 146

Madsen, Sheila K., 145

Management, 21-30
 (*See also* Games, management of)

Master card file of games, 22-24

Materials
 commercial, 54-55, 72, 74, 81
 construction, (*see* Constructing games)
 designing (*see* Constructing games)
 student-made, 55-56
 teacher-made, 43-58
 volunteer-made, 56-58

Metzner, Seymour, 146-147

Miller, Donald C., 144

Modifying games, 9, 25-26, 43-57, 52-55

Mulac, Margaret E., 147

Musselman, Virginia W., 147

Organizing games for learning, 13-30
 (*See also* Games, curriculum)

Packaging, 50-54

Pangle, Mary Ann, 144

Parents
 attitudes toward learning games, 13-15
 helping with games construction, 56-58

Passive games, 3, 61-89

Peer learning, 2, 17-18, 20, 72

Poole, Deanne, 44

Purpose
 for using learning games, 5-11
 parent awareness, 13-15
 student awareness, 15-16

Record-keeping, 22-26, 35-40
 diagnosis, 35-39
 self-evaluation, 39-40

Games As Learning Tools

Relay games, 90-92; chart, 93, 101, 104, 112, 115, 123, 126, 135, 138

Rules for games (*see* Games, directions)

Scheduling games for learning activities, 16-20

Schwartz, Mary, 88

Selection (*see* Games, selection)

Self-direction, 8-11

Self-evaluation, 8-11, 15, 26-27, 39-40, 92

Self-selection, 8-11, 16, 20, 26-27

Sharp, Richard M., 147

Sharp, Vicki F., 147

Simulation games, 4

Solza, Anita C., 147

Spache, Evelyn, B., 147

Spice Series, 148

Storing games, 50-54

Sullivan, Dorothy D., 6, 7, 12, 32, 100-101, 145, 148

Summary game charts by grade level and subjects
  active, 93
  bingo, 63
  board games, 89
  card games, 73
  checkers, 77
  circle games, 93
  concentration, 80
  dominoes, 84
  relay games, 93
  tag and other games, 93

Tag games, 90-92; chart, 93, 101, 104, 113, 123, 136

Task cards, 3, 25-26, 85

Taylor, Bettye K., 145

Teacher-directed games, 16, 19

Teacher evaluation, 8-9, 16-17, 92
  (*See also* Diagnosis)

Teacher-made games, 1, 41-58

Teacher-student evaluation
  (*see* Conferences)

Thomason, Mary E., 148

Thompson, Richard A., 148

Time schedules, 16-20

Tupa, Robbie, 144

Vocabulary games, 95, 99-108; chart, 98

Volunteers, 13-14, 56-58

Wagner, Guy, 149

Waynant, Louise F., 9, 12, 149

Wilson, Robert M., 5, 9, 12, 149

Word analysis games, 95, 121-131; chart, 120

Workshops for constructing games
  parents, 56-58
  teachers, 56-58